"Second Chance at Your Dream *will introduce you to ways to enliven your life and wake up to the possibilities that are inherent in everyone.*"

—Larry Dossey, MD, best-selling author of *Healing Words* and *The Power of Premonitions*

"*The age of audacious aging has arrived. I have always been amazed at how consistently energy work helps people look and feel younger rather than older. No one can combine aging, creativity and energy therapy like Dorothea Hover-Kramer. This guide gives you indispensable tools from-the-trenches for blooming into a passionate and engaged elder with the energy to grow old gloriously.*"

—David Gruder, Ph.D., D.CEP, psychologist, award-winning self-improvement author and Founding President of the Association for Comprehensive Energy Psychology

"*Since time immemorial, humans have been searching for the fountain of youth. This book is the next best thing—a fountain of information about how to maintain the energy and vitality of youth to match the wisdom of maturity, not just physically, but emotionally and spiritually as well. Its author clearly walks her talk and is a living example that this stuff works!*"

—Anodea Judith, Ph.D. best-selling author of *Eastern Body, Western Mind and Waking the Global Heart*

"Second Chance *offers us new perspectives on practical and creative ways to find our own personal Fountains of Youth and to deal with pain and mortality as we get older. Its how-to approach extends our vision and hope. If you've not explored energy psychology before, this book will be a good beginning.*"

—Robert L. Hilliard, Ph.D., former Chief of Public Broadcasting, Federal Communications Commission

"We each choose, why, how, where and when we engage in our world. For the sake of the kids—don't miss your opportunity. This book offers new ideas for your journey."

—Carla B. Johnston, educator, author, and elected public official

"...[this book] invites the reader to re-discover the humanness in us all, the playfulness, and creative self that in so many becomes neglected during the productive years and even more so during the second half of life. Dorothea gives us a new vibrant look at aging, re-discovering the golden years in a new light, infusing them with a new spirit of hope, wisdom and creativity. Beautifully written, to be enjoyed by all."

—Maria J. Becker, MD, FRCP(C), Psychiatrist

"Dorothea Hover-Kramer is a master communicator and therapist who will help you unlock what everyone is striving for—happiness, fulfillment, and health. Second Chance at Your Dream is a blueprint for building a life worth living."

—Barbara Dossey, PhD, RN, author of Florence Nightingale: Mystic, Visionary and Healer and Holistic Nursing: A Handbook for Practice

"You can know now what you didn't know then and have a chance to do it over again! Second Chance at Your Dream clearly guides your discovery in using the energy flowing through you to create the fulfillment of lifelong wellbeing. Truly enlightening!"

—Gregory Nicosia, Ph.D., D.CEP., psychologist, President of the Association for Comprehensive Energy Psychology

"An indispensable package of wisdom—a 'Diagnostics, Service, Maintenance, and Operators Manual' for the rest of your life, regardless of age. If you really want to change your life for the better, read and 'work' this book!"

—Bob and Gloria Ziller, semi-retired computer graphics professionals

"Second Chance at Your Dream *offers new perspectives on a youth oriented society which fails to view every life phase as a gift. Connecting a wide range of topics and weaving personal stories and cultural anecdotes with healing modalities and restorative facts, the book presents fascinating insights about aging and contemporary life.*

Readers will find some chapters more personally relevant, but all should find this author's writing to be positive, validating, reassuring and filled with exciting challenges and new possibilities."

—Olivia Taylor-Young, author of *The Child Snatchers* and columnist

"Dr. Hover-Kramer chose the best title for her fine book: Second Chance at Your Dream. *As one who is advancing in the rapidly growing aged population, I often regret my reduced capacity to accomplish tasks, remember names, bend over, stand up, etc. 'Dr. Dorothea' has applied her wide experience to developing this well-organized guide for aging with sparkle instead of regret. This book does not sermonize about what attitudes you should have—rather it gives concrete steps that bring together the physical and spiritual components to refresh your capacity to expand your life in all its promise."*

William M. ("Mott") Mondale, retired program specialist, National Education Association

"Second Chance at Your Dream *does just what it purports to do. It allows readers opportunity for introspection and analysis of aspects of their lives and then encourages ways to overcome less than optimal responses to stressors—real or perceived. This is a must-read for anyone in the second half of life."*

—Lynn Keegan, Ph.D. RN, AHN-BC, FAAN, past President of the American Holistic Nurses Association

Second Chance at Your Dream

Engaging Your Body's Energy Resources for Optimal Aging, Creativity, and Health

Dorothea Hover-Kramer, EdD, RN, CNS, DCEP
www.SecondChanceDream.com

Energy Psychology Press
Santa Rosa, CA 95403
www.energypsychologypress.com

Library of Congress Cataloging-in-Publication Data

Hover-Kramer, Dorothea
    Second chance at your dream : engaging your body's energy resources for
optimal aging, creativity, and health / by Dorothea Hover-Kramer — 1st ed.
        p. cm.
    Includes bibliographical references and index.
    ISBN: 978-1-60415-038-4
    1. Older people—Psychology. 2. Older people—Life skills guides.
3. Aging—Psychological aspects. 4. Retirement—Planning. 5. Self-
management—Psychology. 6. Energy psychology. 7. Energy medicine.
I. Title.
    HQ1061.H587 2009
    155.67'2—dc22

                        2008044803
        Copyright © 2008–2009, Dorothea Hover-Kramer

Cover design by Victoria Valentine
Typesetting by Karin Kinsey
Editing by Stephanie Marohn
Typeset in ITC Galliard and Eva
Printed in USA
First Edition

10 9 8 7 6 5 4 3 2 1

With Love to All Who Seek to Grow
Throughout Their Entire Lives

And for my Extended Family

Siblings—Luise, Franz, Elenor
Pioneering paths in their seventies and eighties

My adult children and their partners—Karen & Francois, Franz &
Susie, Anne & Mark
Mastering the thirties and forties

My grandchildren—Jesse, Henry, Ben, Sylvia, Mackenzie, Jared,
and Tatum
Exploring life in the first and second decades

And most vitally, my loving life partner, Chuck Kramer

Contents

List of Exercises

Acknowledgments

In writing this book I am reminded of the lifetime of helpful support that has come to me from my many generous teachers, mentors, colleagues, and friends. Although they are too numerous to name here, most of them are visible in the endorsements and the references given in the chapter notes and the recommendations for further reading. I especially want to thank the nurturance of the organizations with which I have had the privilege of working: the American Holistic Nurses Association (AHNA), the Healing Touch Program (HTP), and the Association for Comprehensive Energy Psychology (ACEP). Without the steady encouragement of these wonderful organizations, their fine leadership, and their members, I would not have stretched beyond my limitations to new horizons and enjoyed the richness of several decades of networking.

I also want to thank the many clients who have enriched my life and encouraged me to keep seeking better answers to help relieve their pain and distress. Their stories are an integral part of this book although names and identifying circumstances have been changed for confidentiality. Each of you has brought opportunities for learning and I hope this book is a token of appreciation to you and others in need of healing.

In today's pressure-filled world it is difficult to find a publisher, let alone one who so wholeheartedly encourages the author as Dawson Church does. He and his staff have been untiring in getting the book to press and in integrating all the necessary steps along the way. I especially want to thank assistant Deburah Tribbey as well as copyeditor Stephanie Marohn, layout designer Karin Kinsey, Jeff Anderson and Jennifer Geronimo.

SECOND CHANCE AT YOUR DREAM

Olivia Taylor-Young helped with the initial editing and in affirming I could write this book for her generation.

Photo credits go to Bob Ziller for the author photo and to Luminaria and Kevin Goyer and Gloria and Bob Ziller for the photographs about techniques.

Finally, to my dedicated husband who kept meals and computers going, my most sincere appreciation and hugs.

Introduction

In the second half of life, after your roots have gone deeply into the world,
it is time to reclaim and live...your dream.
—Angeles Arrien

We are born with possibilities. As we grow, we imagine a great dream for our lives. This dream can get submerged or even derailed by the many challenges of adult life. The second half of life, usually beginning sometime after fifty, may offer a second chance.

When we find the courage to grow emotionally and spiritually after midlife, a great adventure opens up. A miracle happens. The fully scheduled or employed person may begin to ease off and play more. Mentoring, grandparenting, or connecting with extended families offers the joys of being with younger people minus the burdens of career juggling and child rearing. If we're fortunate, vacations and future plans begin to take shape around personal wishes rather than what is most convenient or cost effective. The personality can expand, deepen, strengthen, and soften.

Casey worked as a business administrator and raised her two children single-handedly. Although she functioned well, Casey felt incomplete; her life seemed to be passing by in a rather perfunctory, humdrum way. When she turned sixty, she decided to retire on a slim budget and left her busy life in a northern industrial city for a small home in the South. Walking on the beach, with her toes in the cooling water, she spent many hours musing about the quiet time she had chosen. She asked herself, "What now? What else is there to do? What would give me a sense of purpose?"

After six months, Casey realized sitting back and joining clubs would not satisfy her lifelong dream of making a difference in the world. She noticed fertilizer runoff in the tidal basins emptying into the sea and began asking questions about its effects on the beach she so loved. Her questions brought her to a city hall meeting where several friends were in attendance. They found out there was a vacant seat on the city council. With encouragement from her friends, Casey offered to fill the vacancy temporarily. Since she had a strong business sense and empathic ways of relating to others, she was appointed by the council to be their mayor within a year. Because of her sense of fairness, she won the next two elections for mayor and then was elected to be a county commissioner when she turned seventy.

Casey observes, "Retirement gave me the opportunity to revamp my life and to live my dream. I had no idea my calling would be in politics, but this is as good a place as any to make a difference. I was needed. I am more alive and busy now than when I was at my job—and I love my crazy life."

The freedom that comes from having enough time and adequate financial resources permits many to find satisfying new careers or involvements in the second half of life. We have opportunity to return to our goals and ideals with renewed intention and creativity. This book is about specific ways of honing intention and creativity by engaging your body's energy system.

"I Don't Want to Get Old!"

The Greek philosopher Plato observed two great mysteries about humanity: One, no one believes they will ever grow old; and two, no one believes they will ever die. Both beliefs still remain a vast human mystery. Odds are 100 percent against both immortality and not growing older. Each year we live does indeed make us older, although there seems to be a good bit of denial around the idea of becoming "old." Unless you are over a hundred or entertaining like Irving Berlin or George Burns, there doesn't seem to be much humor around aging either.

Few seem to enjoy the second half of life quite as fully as proposed by the media or well-meaning younger people. The "golden years" are often tarnished by another set of demands or emotional withdrawal from life's challenges. Negative beliefs about aging coupled with pervasive discouragement and increasingly limited activity characterize the lives of many elders.

American culture avoids discussing the possibility of creative, positive aging. Anxiety is associated with later life and its four most discernible tasks:

- Retirement from work or change in one's lifestyle.

- Becoming a mentor for others, a steward of the environment, and possibly a grandparent.

- Coping with natural changes in the physical body.

- Losing loved ones and facing one's own mortality.

Inherent cultural prejudices favoring youth and consumerism readily show when there is the least bit of stress. Whereas other cultures and traditions honor elders and give them special status, the West seems to do its best to deny the presence of elders.

My thesaurus told me "oldness" is associated with declining: winter, senectitude, ancientry, antiquity, dotage, senility, decay, decrepitude, loneliness, debility, infirmity—all quite depressing. I started asking my friends over the age of sixty about their thoughts, beliefs, and fears. I told them, "I'm planning to write a book on creativity and longevity." Some were interested, but several stated something like: "I don't want longevity...I don't want to live long, especially if I will be infirm...I just don't want to get old!" Since there is no known way to stop the clock, I began seriously exploring how one could build an innovative lifestyle to stretch beyond cultural norms surrounding aging.

America's Largest Power Group

A subtle but increasingly evident shift in perceptions about aging began in 2005, the year the first of the large American demographic post-war bulge known as the "baby boomers" turned sixty. Advertising began to show successful seniors generating glamorous lifestyles with all the trimmings of the consumer society: gorgeous homes, fine cars, fashionable clothes, and good face creams. At a deeper level, it was becoming less politically correct to deride someone older than oneself or to let prejudices toward the elderly show.

But how many people really look forward to the additional thirty or fifty years that recent advances in medical care have given them? How many shy away from telling their age for fear they'll be marginalized? How many are surprised, even irritated, to receive notice they've reached fifty and are eligible for AARP? Friends confess they avoid reading or toss out AARP's publications. Unfortunately, they may also miss participating in the largest potential power group in America. Accepting ourselves in the second half of life requires acknowledging our nation's demographic reality, with all its gifts and challenges. More than that, it requires a careful look at ourselves to increase self-care and refocus on the big dream for our lives.

AARP turned fifty years old in 2008, along with Caroline Kennedy and Jamie Lee Curtis, among other celebrities. Articles in *AARP* magazine offer insights and wisdom to inspire positive elder lifestyles. In an *AARP* magazine interview, Jamie Lee muses, "Getting older means paring yourself down to an essential version of yourself." In her fun-loving way, she enacts this symbolically by wearing bright ribbon trappings, symbolic of her fetters and defenses, over a black leotard. Then she sheds the fetters one by one, peeling away the layers until only her essence is left.[1]

Notions of aging are changing. We have been given the gift of time. It is imperative that we find ways to use it wisely. More than 30 percent of the population is over fifty, life expectancy averages

85 years,[2] and AARP has thirty-nine million members. Greater than 35 percent of American voters in 2004 were over fifty-five years old, which points to huge potential power held by the nation's mature citizens.[3]

Clearly, it's time for us to look at our lives in affirmative, hopeful terms. Humankind has an incredible ability to invent new patterns of thinking when they are needed. The creative mind knows how to give birth to new forms. Imagine with me the second half of your life as the most productive, prolific, fertile, original, and imaginative part of your existence. Share the excitement of modulating accepted, limiting thought patterns into images of joy, peace, and satisfaction. Because most of us have extra time, we have untold opportunities for creating change within ourselves. And from there, to influence our friends, our communities, and our world.

From Longevity to "Fun-gevity"

My personal journey toward the magical time of "threescore and ten" abounds with adventures, opportunities, losses, and much learning. While raising four teenage children as a single parent, I settled into a psychotherapist's career and directed a large group of colleagues. When the oldest two graduated from high school, I married the brave man who is my present husband. The dream of quiet midlife bliss was shattered one month after the wedding by the accidental death of my oldest son.

At eighteen, Mark was the epitome of a football hero. Full of life, he was also an enthusiastic writer. After repeatedly being voted most valuable player on his high school team, he received a full football scholarship to a large midwestern university. While running on a foggy morning before the freshman season began, he was hit by a truck and died instantly. The whole team was in shock for weeks, and national news media carried the story. I received sympathy cards from nearly all fifty states.

These events dramatically shaped the second half of my life. I started asking questions. What did I need to learn? What gift lay in the juxtaposition of these dramatic life-changing events? Why was my son's bounding energy still so strong? I wanted to learn about energetic connections with loved ones beyond the seeming wall of physical death. I recalled how awareness of human energies had often helped me in times of peril. While living in Berlin after the disastrous end of World War II, I sensed light and color around people who were best able to help me after my mother's death when I was five. I also learned to gently pass my hands over sick birds to speed their recovery.

Later, I chose nursing and planned to use my hands and heart to help those in need as Florence Nightingale seemed to have done. I was somewhat ahead of my time since, until 1970, nursing did not formally acknowledge the possibility of helping patients via human energies. But I was in the right profession to learn more about energetic interventions and to blend them with my later practice as a counseling psychologist.

Leadership positions with the American Holistic Nurses Association (1981 to 1990) led me to assist in organizing Healing Touch, a program for teaching energy modalities to health-care professionals. This resulted in writing several books about the interface between energy concepts and counseling therapies. I became a counseling educator and cofounded the Association for Comprehensive Energy Psychology (ACEP). Many conferences and travel adventures followed.

At the peak of my professional career as a psychologist and president of ACEP, my husband and I decided we would like to retire to a peaceful, remote part of Oregon. Like many people who retire, we guessed at what we might like rather than really knowing what we wanted. It seemed a good idea to slow down and engage in less stressful activities. My walking had diminished to short forays around the house because of a hip problem. I contacted the senior center, studied yoga, joined painting groups, and started doing some of the things for which I had never had time before.

Then, two years ago, I found renewed vitality after receiving a hip replacement. Despite my affection for complementary healing modalities, I came to appreciate Western medicine's fabulous gift of new mobility. Not only can I now walk with ease, but my life has expanded emotionally. With the help of energy exercises continually developing within ACEP, I gained strength to envision active and creative longevity. This new phase of life is now my "fun-gevity" time.

A retirement of withdrawal into quiet seclusion is no longer an option. The dream of a meaningful second half of life calls out. The dream includes being present to my seven grandchildren. We celebrated our lives by moving to a vital community on Washington's Olympic Peninsula and I choose to address major issues affecting the grandchildren's lives such as global uncertainty and environmental destruction. They deserve a vital elder who has time and patience to participate in the social changes needed to uplift our collective consciousness.

I envision a new picture of "audacious aging"[4] in which engaged, passionate elders bring their collective wisdom to our imperiled world. We are the talented and essential beings who, by healing and empowering ourselves, can heal and empower others. We are the ones who bring love of humanity and the natural world to our families and communities. The second half of life is indeed the opportunity to reclaim your life's dream!

No Pills or Harmful Side Effects Here

This book is an invitation to join in the adventure of self-discovery while adding on more birthdays. We'll explore ways to stay in balance, to release dysfunctional patterns, to change perceptions of difficult situations, to build a sense of hope and positive expectancy, to connect with innate creativity, and to align energetically with the soul's purpose and learn to trust intuition. This does not involve some external factor, medication, or device for treating life's challenges. It is all about exploring the resources that are innately yours and readily available.

Within your body resides your vital life force, the quality referred to as *qi* (pronounced "chee") in classical Chinese texts that date back more than five thousand years. This vital life force is the focus of the current practices of acupuncture and acupressure. Directing this *qi* with emotional acupressure (no needles!) by tapping or holding meridian acupoints can assist you in resolving internal conflicts and removing blocks to creativity, thereby empowering you to live more fully.

Contrary to traditional thinking that associates living well with lots of social activity, the full-energy life is about connecting to inner wisdom and refining the arrow of intention. This orientation is filled with joy, peacefulness, openness, curiosity, wonder, appreciation, flexibility, exploration, new viewpoints, and moving "beyond the box" of traditional thinking about aging.

Fun-gevity is made possible by letting go of stressful issues rapidly so there is available energy for more satisfying choices. For most day-to-day issues, the principles of energetic self-care advanced in this book will give excellent opportunities for refocusing. Care of more deep-seated issues may include seeking outside assistance, ideally from a practitioner of energy psychology or other energy therapy (see the resource list at the end of the book). Exercises in each chapter will lead you to find new ways of sustaining energy levels and lightening up inwardly. Like a wide range of colors, the varied exercises will allow you to find the unique palette of exercise patterns that best suits you. The interventions offer drug-free paths for relieving anxiety, finding inner harmony, and thriving in advancing years.

The book is in four parts. They flow from an explanation of the personal energy system to practical applications in addressing specific issues. The first section is your introduction to a conceptual framework of personal energy for becoming more flexible and resourceful. We'll explore cross-cultural resources and cite studies showing how these concepts are well within the realm of current scientific knowledge. Epigenetic research, for example, is demonstrating the power of our thoughts to influence gene expression and hence the body's cellular and DNA structures.

The second part is directly practical. We'll learn releasing maneuvers to use whenever you are shaken by external events. Transforming difficult issues allows more energy for innovative thinking. We'll also rethink beliefs that are no longer functional and find methods of installing more desirable, useful beliefs. Celebrating the present with its unique gifts becomes possible as we learn methods for bringing life-enhancing awareness into every moment.

The third section addresses numerous ways of establishing yourself as the creative artist of your life. Learning from a self-inventory brings focus to inner wisdom with specific steps for developing intuition as a resource for creativity. Accessing transpersonal, spiritual dimensions is another means of expanding originality, and you'll learn to nurture your own inner artist with hope and protective imagery.

The fourth part considers energetic approaches for two of life's greatest challenges: dealing with pain and viewing death from a new perspective. The book closes by redefining personal myths and integrating seemingly dissimilar aspects of our lives into a dancing, dynamic whole.

****

I invite you to imagine and rehearse the life you really want and to enliven your dream goals. I encourage you to develop your own version of creative fun-gevity by employing the suggestions in these chapters. May the journey be richer and more fulfilling than you ever expected!

Part I:
Energy for a Fulfilling Life

Chapter One
The River Wants to Flow!

...the delight, when your courage kindled,
And out you stepped onto new ground,
Your eyes young again with energy and dream,
A path of plenitude opening before you.
—John O'Donohue

Mary and Janet have been friends for more than thirty years. When they met for a recent lunch date, Janet seemed pale and tense. Mary's traditional opening "How are you?" was tinged with genuine concern.

"I'm fine," Janet replied automatically, then hesitantly added, "But I just had a close call on the freeway. Some old fart barely missed crashing into me and I'm still feeling a little shaky."

To soothe her friend's nerves, Mary chimed in, "Old fart? Remember, you're sixty-nine and I'm seventy-one." Chuckling, they recalled George Bernard Shaw's saying "Old age is always twenty years older than you are" and agreed "old" for them must mean ninety—or later.

As the friends chatted and enjoyed their lunch, Janet's life-threatening incident dropped into the background and her taut shoulder muscles relaxed. Gradually, she returned to her normal self.

Later, I will address beliefs and prejudices surrounding the word "old." But first, let's focus on the emotional disturbance of Janet's near-accident and the cumulative effects of life-threatening stressors.

Further on, we'll also consider ways of changing encrusted beliefs and resolving everyday issues with the body's energy resources.

Out of Kilter

Brief, traumatic incidents are very real human experiences. Often, they leave us feeling out of sorts and imbalanced. Even the most focused individuals will have experiences causing disorientation and distress. In someone who is basically emotionally healthy, such turmoil may soon pass and be forgotten. If the pressure is unrelenting, however, or if the person leads an otherwise stress-filled life, it may take considerably longer to unwind from the shaky feeling Janet described.

If intense stress is repeated often or continuously (for many days or weeks), health changes such as high blood pressure, frequent headaches, or fatigue can set in. In addition, emotional disturbances such as ongoing anxiety or a quiet sense of despair become internalized as stressors keep piling up. It's important to remember there are many dimensions of distress. The more obvious stress is one of too much to do with too little time, but another is the stress engendered by having too little meaningful activity. The latter results in boredom and underuse of one's resources. The buildup of either stress with its effects on human energy levels is all too familiar in our culture. Recent statistics report over 75 percent of all physical illnesses are stress related and that one in three American adults is depressed or anxious. Antidepressants and tranquilizers are the most frequently prescribed drugs on the market. The percentage and incidence are higher among those in life's later decades because stress has a cumulative effect over time.

All of us have had a jarring experience that left us exhausted and/ or in pain for several days, even though medical examination showed no broken bones or physical injury. Something subtler happened, something not treatable with medication or procedures known to Western medicine. One way of understanding this condition is to say that more subtle energies, or the energy body, absorbed the impact of the trauma and, as a result, became distorted, imbalanced, blocked, or depleted in some way.

Popular language reflects understanding of changes in energy levels. For example, we often hear statements such as "I feel charged (with energy)" or "I feel depleted (of energy), or "I feel scattered... fragmented...pulled...or...pushed." These approximate the true condition of the energy body at any given moment.

For most people, energetic disturbance occurs frequently, perhaps several times a day. It can be sensed as a tired, depleted feeling with vague discomfort in the entire body. It can, in fact, be assessed by health-care professionals who have studied Therapeutic Touch, Healing Touch, Reiki, or some of the other well-known energy therapies. "Energy field disturbance" is recognized as an accepted nursing diagnosis[1] and guides caregivers to rebalance human energies with specific techniques.

Coming Back "Online"

Understanding energetic imbalance as a distortion of the energy body leads us to seek relevant remedies. For example, people say, "I need to recharge my batteries" or "I want to refocus myself" or "I must pull myself together." Although recognizing imbalance and stating intention for relief is helpful, focused activity is needed to renew one's inner vitality.

Here are two exercises[2] to relieve energy field disturbance such as the one that impacted Janet.

Exercise 1.1 Centering

1. While sitting comfortably, release the breath fully with a sigh, or as if you're blowing out a candle. Do this two to three times more while imaging stress and tension flowing out through your

hands and feet. The in-breath will naturally be deeper as you proceed.

2. Allow yourself to imagine a peaceful place in nature—seeing, hearing, feeling, even smelling it. Let the peacefulness fill your body with light and warmth. Continue to release any tension or emotional distress with each breath.

3. After five to ten minutes, notice how you feel and jot down any images or ideas that came to you. Notice that your breathing has deepened and any other changes such as relief of muscle tension in your body.

Exercise 1.2 The Brush Down

1. As you think of a recent stressful event, set your intention to release its effects. While sitting or standing, take a deep breath and then let the breath go, fully releasing pressure and tension. Imagine giving it to the earth to be healed and cleansed. Again, breathe and exhale to let any remaining tension flow out through your hands and feet.

2. Next, bring your hands above your head on the in-breath and breathe out fully while gently brushing downward with hands on inch or more above the body, head to toe. Allow a sigh or groan to help release the tension fully as the hands move downward.

Hands above the head in "The Brush Down"

3. Continue releasing with each out-breath while brushing with one hand from under each arm, then alternating to the other side. Then brush with both hands down the upper and lower back, the groin area, and the inside of your legs. Imagine you are smoothing the ruffled edges of your energy field.

4. Notice how you feel after three to five minutes of this execise.

Allow yourself to use one these exercises each morning when you first arise to soften the transition into the day. Also, remember to use one when something nerve-wracking happens, such as getting caught in a traffic jam or feeling pressured. Experience will prove which exercise is most helpful in restoring your vitality quickly.

Other Blocks to Energy Flow

In the second half of life, people often become interested in the lives of famous and/or successful seniors—elders who live a long time, continue being highly creative, seem unshaken by declines in health, and overcome incredible obstacles. Are they superheroes? How do they really do it?

Wondering about this, many people notice the futility of their internal pep talks and inability to make goal-setting, positive thinking, friendly advice, and examples from the stars work for them. The flow of inner vitality can become impeded in the second half of life unless major shifts occur.

For discussion in this book, I use the metaphor of energy flowing like a river around and through the body. This flow sends instant communication to vital organs and hormones, regulates cellular integrity, and brings liveliness to every chosen activity. Just as a fallen branch or tree can obstruct the flow of a river, patterns of belief and automatic thinking can block the flow of inspiring, life-giving energy. Behind the obstructions, stagnant pools build up. Over time, less and less movement occurs as sludge gathers and further clogs the water flow pathways. In addition to energy system disruption by a traumatic event, blockages to psychological energy flows become apparent in the form of limiting or dysfunctional beliefs[3] and repeated ineffective responses to daily stressors. Interventions to change direction by breaking down or removing impediments are needed.

Pete believed in control. As a retired school superintendent he knew the value of structure to contain what he called "the herds of unruly children" under his direction. After retiring from his stressful job, Pete transferred his controlling tendencies to regulating his wife, their joint money, and her participation in the senior community where they lived. He became convinced she was looking for a younger man and even hid the car keys so she could not leave home. She came to therapy to find relief from "Parsimonious Pete." Fortunately, he also became curious about changing the circumscribed life he had created.

The vast barriers Pete had built up revolved around his core belief that no one could be trusted. The power of this belief caused not only stagnation but also misery. With careful attention to ways of building trust, Pete's therapist gently led him to find more functional beliefs such as "Not everyone is an unruly child," "My wife is trustworthy," and "I can safely take small steps to reach out to others." Pete's therapist then helped him to strengthen the shift in perception by having him touch specific energy points (acupoints) on his body to release the old patterns and embed new, more effective thinking styles.

Here's a sample resource to help shift one of your limiting beliefs by gently holding or tapping one of the body's energy points.

Exercise 1.3 Changing a Limiting Mindset

1. Think of a belief you currently have about aging. Rate the truth of the belief on a scale of 1 to 10 (1 means it's barely true for you, 2–6 means it's pretty frustrating and bothers you, 7–10 means it really makes you dislike yourself or others for believing it).

2. Take a deep breath and release it fully. Think of the belief in its possible worst format and briefly connect with the feeling generated in you. (Examples: "Getting old is hell," "Aging is difficult," and "Eventually, you'll lose everything.")

3. Let the right hand touch the tender spot below the collarbone and halfway down the left side of the chest. (This is one of several neurolymphatic reflex points; rubbing them often produces a soothing, calming effect.) Gently rub in small circles toward the left shoulder.

Rubbing a neurolymphatic reflex point to change a limiting mindset.

4. While rubbing the tender spot state, "Even though I sometimes think_____, I deeply and profoundly honor and accept myself." (Fill in the blank with your belief, such as "Getting old is hell.") Repeat at least three times to bring full awareness of the message to your system.

5. Now follow with a more empowering belief while again rubbing the tender spot. (Examples: "I can make the second half of life

as creative and fun as I wish," I'm not doomed, I'm the choice-maker," and "I can attract the resources I need to help me.")

6. Rate how true the limiting belief is on your scale, and note how true the new belief is for you. Notice how you feel inside. Repeat the exercise as often as needed to reprogram the mind-body connections.

In addition to revising long-held beliefs, resolving temporary conflicts within oneself or with others is a much-needed skill. Using resources within the body's energy system can help to release a negative emotion so the mind is fully available for problem solving.

Ginny was constantly irritated by the men's noisy pool table games at her community center. One day she decided she had to speak out on behalf of the many women who enjoyed doing needlework in the same large hall. She began by talking to herself and affirming she did not need to be angry to assert herself. When she was calmer, Ginny was able to organize her thoughts, gather several allies from the sewing group, and speak in a firm, logical manner to the leader of the men's group. The result was renewed understanding from the men and an invitation to join in the planning for their upcoming square dance.

Here's a brief exercise to reduce the intensity of a feeling and to clear the mind to help resolve a problem.

Exercise 1.4 Releasing a Strong Negative Feeling

1. Think of a recent event that generated a strong feeling within you. Rate the intensity of the feeling on a scale of 1 to 10 (1 meaning not very strong, 3–6 meaning quite strong, and 7+ meaning it really agitates you or even reminds you of a prior life-threatening event).

2. Gently tap or hold where the eyebrow meets the nose. If possible, use both hands to alternately and slowly tap this point 10 to 15 times. Take a deep breath and let it go.

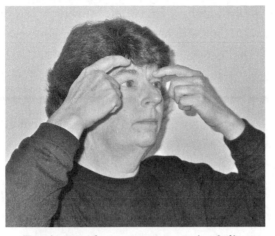

Tapping to release a strong negative feeling.

3. Thinking of the event again, gently tap or hold at the outer eye, on the bony orbit, in the same way while thinking of the belief. Take a deep breath and release fully.

4. Gently tap or hold the point under the nose while thinking for a moment about the belief. Take another deep releasing breath.

5. Gently tap or hold both sides of the collarbone points just below the clavicle near the "notch" in the middle of the upper sternum. Take another releasing breath.

6. Gently tap or hold the side of each hand, on the "karate chop" point. (If you turn the hands slightly, you can use one hand against the other to tap on both points simultaneously.) Take a deep breath and relax.

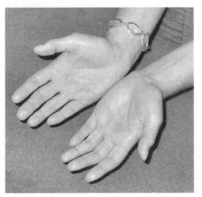

Hold one hand against the other at the Karate Chop point.

7. Affirm "Even though ___(Example: this terrible event has happened) or "Even though (Example: someone was unpleasant to me), I still deeply and profoundly honor and accept myself." Repeat several times using your own words but keeping the intention of the message.

8. Note how you feel now in relation to the problem event and rate the intensity on the 1–10 scale.

Traumatic events, constricting beliefs, and strong negative emotions create an imprint or constriction that impedes the flow of energetic messaging in the body. The exercises in this chapter give you basic resources for:

- Handling sudden jarring events that impact the whole energy system.

- Recognizing and revising limiting belief patterns.

- Releasing negative emotions related to current life events so you can access better options.

These tools will be helpful as we find avenues for a full-energy life. The intention is to open your energy flow, release blockages, and experience your vitality more fully.

Other than increased oxygen from taking deeper breaths and possible inner calming, you may not notice dramatic changes right away. As with a physical exercise routine or taking vitamins, the effects of self-care interventions may become more evident when repeated regularly over several weeks or months. In time, however, you may also notice increased self-esteem and personal effectiveness. One person who employed these methods for several weeks observed, "I feel as if I can handle whatever challenges come my way. I'm more confident; I don't feel quite so helpless or unwanted anymore."

To conclude, let's engage in a quick life review. Self-discovery is at the heart of change and can guide you toward a nonjudgmental, self-caring path to achieving higher levels of well-being.

Exercise 1.5 Quick Life Review

1. Note what you're already doing that has engendered a positive outlook and works for you: _____

    _____

2. List the life goals you still want to achieve: _____

    _____

3. Note what seems to hold you back from expressing who you really are: _____

    _____

4. Note something irrational in yourself such as unrealistic expectations of yourself or others, dependence on substances to make you feel good, or indulgence in diversions and "time killers" such as excessive TV or video watching and computer or card games: _____

    _____

5. Ask yourself how you usually handle negative emotions: _____

    _____ and how you would like

    things to be different: _____

    _____

6. Note if you have retired from life prematurely or settled for less than an optimal life: _____

    _____

7. Note how you handle surprises, upsets, and change: _____

    _____

    _____

8. Note what you do that brings joy, play, and the spirit of laughter into your everyday life: _____

    _____

As you look at the review, honor your willingness to explore new possibilities for yourself. Deeply respect your wish for a fuller life.

* * * *

In the next two chapters, we'll explore the theories and science supporting the idea of engaging healthy energy flows in your body. Further on, we'll look at many ways to establish balance between activity and rest and between reaching out and going within— the skills needed to restore and optimize the vital energies of your being.

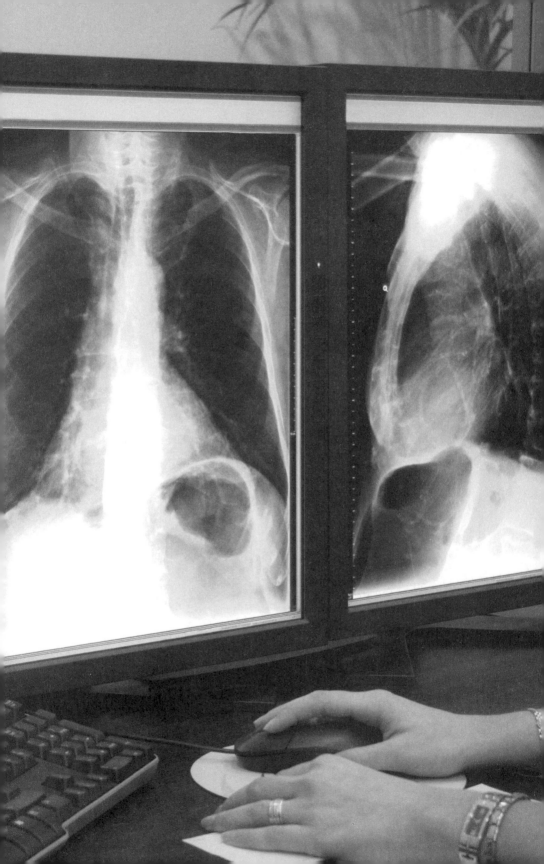

Chapter Two
What Science Knows About Human Energies

We will never understand the scientific basis of everything. We must be open to approaches that work even when we don't understand how or why they work.

—National Institutes of Health administrator
Ralph Snyderman

The personal optimism inherent in energy approaches— "You can learn to help yourself by activating your energy resources"—creates a beacon of hope for the most desperate situations. Although we do not yet fully understand all the dynamics of psychologically oriented energetic interventions, remarkable changes have been documented over the past twenty years. Relief from severe emotional distress abounds in the clinical reports of energy therapists. Chronic pain and its emotional burdens are diminished or rendered more manageable. An anxious person becomes able to decrease worrying and consider other options. Those who held long-term resentments and grudges are able to forgive and move forward. Phobias seem to disappear, never to return. Severely traumatized individuals experience decrease in the emotional intensity of their trauma and become able to access new understanding about themselves and the world around them.[1]

After your experience with the exercises in chapter 1, you may be wondering if these ideas have been studied and validated. What is actually known from science and research about human energies?

Since scientific evidence can be quite complex, this chapter explores some of the most relevant material and leaves it to you to seek out desired additional information from the resources given in the chapter notes. First, we will explore understandings of human energies as currently known in medicine, physics, and biology, and then review some of the most relevant research about energy psychology. Whenever the content seems a bit dense, you may wish to rub your two collarbone points,on each side of the notch on the top of your ribcage known as "brain buttons," to refresh your vitality.

Vibrational Medicine

Scientists describe their understanding of the universe through theoretical models. While infallible proof of many major theories, such as the mechanics of subatomic particle interactions, are not fully available as yet, theories give us fascinating metaphors for increased understanding and for making inferences about the nature of reality. The concept of human energies as a flowing river with possible constrictions and impediments gives us one useful model for comprehending what may actually occur when energetic interventions are used to release congestion. Other, more effective models, theories, and inferences will likely replace this model in the future.

Understanding how energy moves in the body is facilitated by insights about the electrical and magnetic nature of the human organism. The practice of Western medicine is becoming increasingly vibrational, or energetic. Electromagnetic theory and its practical application is the framework for many of the current innovative practices in Western medicine, including mainstream diagnostic and treatment procedures.

Gone are the days when dangerous dyes had to be given to study kidney function or skulls had to be cut open to diagnose a circulatory problem or tumor. For diagnosis, there is now a variety of noninvasive scanners, such as CT (computerized tomography), PET (positron emission tomography), and MRI (magnetic resonance

imaging), that give feedback about molecular exchange in soft tissue. These sophisticated scans demonstrate areas of constriction
or obstruction interfering with healthy patterning in cells and soft
tissue.[2] The EKG (electrocardiogram) and EEG (electroencepha-
logram) are two well-known diagnostic tools for measuring the
natural electrical rhythms of the heart and brain. Newer resources,
the EMC (electromagnetic cardiogram) and EME (electromagnetic
encephalogram), measure the magnetic outputs of the heart and
brain, providing more accurate details of subtle changes in these
vital organs than can be obtained by electrical measurements alone.
SQUID (superconducting quantum interference device) technology
establishes the parameters of the human biofield, which surrounds
the body and is used to evaluate the body's relative strength. This
scan helps to determine bilateral damage occurring from a cerebral
vascular accident or stroke.

Similar to diagnostic processes, treatments are becoming less
invasive as comprehension of electromagnetic interactions within
the human body increases. In the 1960s, orthopedic surgeon Robert
Becker began to explore electrical circuitry of the body to understand nonunion problems in complex bone fractures. He identified
numerous slight direct currents of electricity which flow throughout
the body. He found they reversed their polarity, or direction, at the
site of an injury. When this "current of injury" was supported with
a small amount of electrical stimulation, bone healing accelerated.
Over several decades, Becker mapped out an energetic grid of the
human body that paralleled the nervous system but is electromagnetic and nonmaterial in nature.[3] He surmised this system's function was to send information to all parts of the human organism,
even in the presence of neural damage such as that from strokes or
other major bodily trauma. Thus he suggested the presence of dual
information systems: the nervous system with its many physical components, and the subtle energy system. The latter consists of numerous electrical circuits, and we can infer it to be a form of natural

redundancy that exists to ensure continued messaging to vital organs and tissue in case of injury.

Today we see medicine continuing to use energy concepts in diagnosing and treating illness. Current treatments include high-frequency sound waves to break up kidney stones, focused radiation to pinpoint specific cancers, electricity to alleviate pain and shrink tumors, electromagnetic fields to stimulate fracture healing, laser surgery to minimize tissue damage, and magnetic fields to alleviate the pain and inflammation of arthritis. All of these new approaches build on the body's self-healing capacities through feedback loops believed to promote cellular repair and reorganization.

Further explorations in modern medicine take seriously the presence of differing electromagnetic frequencies in the body. The frequency of the physical body is different from the energy body (or biofield) but coexists within the same space in your body and being. Current explorations suggest the acupoint/meridian system is a discreetly organized network that seems to connect both physical and energetic frequencies. We can infer that it sends messages from the environment to nerves, muscles, blood vessels, and deeper organs. The chakras are believed to be specialized centers of the energy body, each associated with major nerve centers and glands. We infer, from successful interventions using them, that they act as transformers to modify energy from the universe and stimulate hormonal, nerve, and cellular activity.[4]

The energy resources of the body can also be used to bring about balance and healing as suggested in the self-care exercises in this book. As we work with these fascinating energy-oriented interventions, healing and well-being increase dramatically. In fact, many physicians now encourage patients to explore energy therapies as part of conventional medical care although empirical research confirmations are still at early stages.

Quantum Interrelationships

The presence of subtle energy was first proposed by famed physicist Albert Einstein to describe the minute, ongoing interrelationships between subatomic particles. The presence of invisible, nonmaterial energies is currently confirmed by particle astrophysicists who report that at least 95 percent of the universe is made up of "dark energy and matter."[5] Translated into human terms, our vital life force, *qi* or *prana,* is likely a form of this very stuff of the universe. *Qi* continuously interacts with matter as seen in the many ongoing and subtle interactive components of the body. Many puzzles remain in physics, such as: How does energy become matter, how does energy influence matter, and how do some subatomic particles attract mass to become increasingly heavier atoms while others seem to dissipate into other forms of energy-like particles?

Einstein's famous equation for the interrelationship between energy and matter ($E = mc^2$) predicted the existence of energy beyond the known constant of the speed of light. This magnetoelectrical energy has extremely high frequencies and is not yet measurable. It is known to exist within the ten-dimensional model of the universe currently conceptualized by many physicists.[6]

Matter, energy, and human consciousness are profoundly interconnected. Innovative physicists such as William Tiller suggest the human organism consists of interactive vibrations of differing frequencies that constitute our subtle energy body. This is akin to the patterns in the universe described as a succession of vibrating particles or "strings." These particles vibrate at different speeds, ranging from very low frequencies to exceedingly rapid ones exceeding the speed of light. What is visible to the human eye is but a small section of the vast energy vibrations of the known electromagnetic spectrum.

The advent of quantum mechanics toward the end of the twentieth century superseded many of Einstein's theories and demonstrated a world of remarkable interconnectedness. Bell's theorem (published by physicist John S. Bell in 1964) proposed the interrelationship of subatomic particles to each other over vast distances and time and was later confirmed in Swiss experiments.[7] Much of the presumed science of cause and effect is reshaped when seen through the lens of quantum mechanical physics. Nonlinear inconsistencies such as the dual nature of light, which functions as either particle or wave under different circumstances, are accepted as being part of a larger whole not yet fully understood. Quantum mechanics also helps to explain studies which demonstrate how subatomic particles can be influenced by human consciousness.[8]

The possibility of minute changes in electron structures that may influence a whole system to change and access new probabilities is easily seen in the nonlinear dynamic of worldwide weather. For example, the influence of slight temperature shifts on ocean currents is now well integrated in weather prediction meteorology and ongoing discussions of El Niño and La Niña effects. On the human scale, a single psychological insight or "aha!" can bring about numerous emotional shifts and generate breakthrough ideas.

The best-known model of components of subtle human energies consists of the biofield as a whole, the chakras or energy vortices, the meridians with related acupoints, and other interactive, radiant circuits. The presence of these components is confirmed by ongoing studies at the California Institute for Human Science.[9] To give a simple metaphor, the biofield can be likened to the glow of a city seen as one approaches on land or from the air at night; the chakras are a series of vortices resembling smaller urban centers within the city; the meridians are like the city streets with the acupoints marking the intersections, and the overall circuits such as electrical lighting may be likened to the radiant flow pathways. All of these components represent different aspects of one city. Similarly, different aspects of the body's information messaging systems and denser structures such as cells and molecules are part of one whole body.

Science is moving toward more fluid understanding of the myriad delicate interrelationships in nature. Scientists, especially those immersed in quantum mechanics, now speak of perspectives and perceptions rather than objective reality; of creative probabilities instead of outcomes; and of useful metaphors and models rather than definable, permanent truths. Increased knowledge and production of enhanced theories is accelerating daily with computer imagery and modeling. We live in an open-ended, evolving world alive with possibilities, and vastly more complex than realized heretofore.

The Genius of Your Genes

More and more data are showing us specifics about subtle interrelationships in biology as well. Consider, for example, your own body: It is not the same as it was ten years ago; all cells, even those in your brain, have been replaced multiple times, some in several days, some over several months. But, something of you is still the same. Is it a blueprint of some kind? Your consciousness? Your essence?

Consciousness is defined as the total impressions, thoughts, and feelings of an individual. Physicists, biologists, and social scientists all seem to be arriving at the same conclusion: Everything is influenced by the nature of consciousness. We are learning, for example, how focused intent to help ourselves and others can be a powerful force for personal change. In addition, new studies are demonstrating consciousness to be a powerful influence in shaping cellular and genetic structures.

One of the most revealing enterprises showing the interrelationship between consciousness and matter comes from the new science of *epigenetics,* first identified in 2001.[10] This new field within biology focuses on the many signals and sources that either activate or suppress gene expression. Both activation and suppression of gene expression are closely allied with electromagnetic energy flows shaped by intention and consciousness. In other words, epigenetics studies the ways activation of DNA sequences from your genes can be enhanced or impeded by your state of mind. Old notions of "genetic determinism" or ideas that nothing can influence genetic material have been debunked.

Among the many recent studies in genomics, the nature of gene expression and its relationship to human states of mind, is one that demonstrates the effects of Herbert Benson's famed "relaxation response."[11] Although systemic changes with relaxation such as release of muscle tension, increased oxygenation to tissues and organs, and immune system empowerment were well known, the exact mechanisms for these changes at the genetic level were not known. Research now shows that a large number of genes express fully when subjects center and relax. This expression brings wide-ranging effects including immune system activation, effective coping with inflammation, regulation of cellular life and death, and absorption of free radicals. The new research provides the first compelling evidence regarding gene expression results in practitioners of meditation, yoga, focused breathing, prayer, and focused intention. The "hard" science of genomics has met with the "soft" science of psychology and relaxation techniques for an indisputable understanding of the interaction of body and mind.

To give a single example of choices regarding gene expression, consider what happens when you cut your finger. The tissue trauma sends a signal to the genes associated with wound healing. These genes then stimulate malleable stem cells into forming skin replacement cells and creating blood-clotting materials. The signals tell the proteins that are wrapped like sheaths around DNA strands to unwrap and allow wound healing to begin. If there is interference with this signal due to a strong negative emotion such as anger, the signals to the proteins cannot flow easily. The message is garbled or altered because dealing with the emotion diverts your available energy at that moment. Wound healing becomes delayed or compromised as a consequence.

"[E]pigenetic signals suggest a whole new avenue for catalyzing wellness in our bodies," writes author-publisher Dawson Church in his groundbreaking book *The Genie in Your Genes*.[12] The psychological and biological factors involved in stress reactions directly affect gene expression hundreds of times a day. If positive thoughts prevail or allow for quick releases of negativity, genes can express by unwrapping the DNA strands needed for specific cellular healing. If negativity prevails in the form of a limiting belief or by hanging on to resentments, the expression will either be missing, incomplete, or delayed. The fundamental idea of functional genomics is: "Most of our genes are...active players responding quickly, from one moment to the next, to the cues, challenges, and contingencies of our ever-changing daily experience. Our thoughts, emotions, and behavior modulate gene expression in health and optimal performance as well as stress and illness."[13] Our genes are expressed in the continually changing life events we experience, including our dramas, the residue of trauma, and significant life events. They switch on and off like toggle computer signals in response to our conscious efforts to cope with stressors in our external environments as well as our internal wishes, hopes, and dreams.

It stands to reason that epigenetic factors play a significant role in health and optimal aging. A study of 2,700 men over a ten-year period showed those who engaged in regular volunteer activities had significantly lower death rates than those who did not.[14] The study suggests that altruism, in addition to being good for others, is also good for helpers. Noted effects of doing good are reduced stress, improved immune function, and a sense of joy, peace, and well-being. These effects lasted long after the helpful events and increased with the frequency of reaching out to others. The body produces hundreds of feel-good chemicals called endorphins, which relieve pain and mitigate stress responses such as increased cortisol production. Caring for others apparently helps to generate gene expression that facilitates endorphin production from the body's own pharmacy.

Although human studies have not yet been done, studies of rat brains show differing biochemical and epigenetic responses to stress among well-adjusted rats who groomed their pups and anxious, fearful ones who did not. Stress-dampening responses had greater degrees of expression in happy rats, and happy rats showed higher levels of available biochemicals to bind with the protein sheaths around relevant genes for facilitating gene expression. In the anxious, fearful rats, gene-suppressing substances bonded to DNA strands and inhibited the expression of genes involved in reducing stress.[15]

This work leads us to see ourselves as the ones holding the key to effective gene expression via our attitudes and beliefs. We have the power to select the interests, actions, and lifestyles that nurture gene expression. Each of us is indeed the guiding genius behind our unique pattern of gene expression!

Research into the nature of consciousness and its worldwide influences is ongoing. Consciousness, as we can grasp thus far, is both local and nonlocal; in other words, we have individual self-perceptions as well as experiences of our interconnections. As human beings we are part of a larger whole. Intention—directing our volition and attention to help ourselves and others—is a special form of directed human consciousness Intention, as we'll explore further, is also the direct means for activating the resources of the human energy system.

Research Confirmations

Research confirming the efficacy of energetic interventions such as the ones proposed in this book already exists and is ongoing. Therapeutic Touch, Healing Touch, and energy psychology have their extensive research projects referenced on their websites and continually give updates of projects in process and published reports.[16] Currently, ACEP has twenty-seven research projects under way in relation to meridian therapies and boasts several publications in peer-reviewed journals.[17]

One fascinating recent study involved measuring the effects of Emotional Freedom Techniques (EFT, which employs a brief tapping sequence similar to exercise 1.4) on stress and anxiety. Measurements were taken before and after administering EFT to determine changes in blood levels of cortisol, the detrimental plaque-generating hormone produced by the body when excessive stress is experienced. Implementing EFT brought about a 25 percent decrease in production of the harmful hormone.[18] The results were so surprising and exceeded traditional talk therapy so dramatically that the laboratory repeated the tests several times just to be sure!

Current published research evidence for meridian interventions in energy psychology (EP) demonstrates relief from irrational fear of small animals,[19] increased effectiveness of psychotherapy,[20] and relief of post-traumatic stress disorders.[21] One informal South American study, which included thousands of psychiatric patients suffering from severe anxiety and other disorders, showed 76 percent remission among the subjects after three to five brief treatments with an EP method.[22]

One of England's leading psychiatrists, Dr. Phil Mollon, summarized meridian therapy effects in treating distresses commonly experienced by healthy persons. Resolutions with meridian interventions were more rapid and more effective than with talk therapies. The frequently experienced distresses Dr. Mollon treated with EP included fear, grief, guilt, anger, shame, jealousy, painful memories, loneliness, frustration, and procrastination.[23]

Chakra and biofield interventions studied by Healing Touch (HT) and Therapeutic Touch (TT) researchers consistently demonstrate reduction of pain sensation,[24] increased relaxation,[25] enhanced immune system function,[26] and even accelerated wound healing.[27] Of particular interest is the overall experience of joy and well-being seen in TT and HT practitioners. Since personal centering and energetic self-care are considered essential parts of their healing endeavors, practitioners regularly engage in them. Researcher Janet Quinn measured the enhanced self-efficacy of TT practitioners[28] which is of particular interest to those of us in the second half of life who seek to maintain high quality wellness.

These research projects underscore society's shifting desire to go beyond short-term curing toward a more integrative view of lifelong healing. In 2000, the Office of Alternative Medicine, founded in 1992 within the National Institutes of Health (NIH), expanded to form the National Center for Complementary and Alternative Medicine (NCCAM) as a fully funded, separate division. The growing budget fosters research into complementary modalities such as acupuncture and herbal treatments for depression and arthritis. Investigation of a special category named "frontier medicine" has also been funded to study therapies for which there are no as yet known biological mechanisms, such as energy therapy approaches.

Multimodal centers for integrative medicine and healing arts are available nationwide to address not only physical illness but also its psychological and spiritual components. The development of holistic and integrative emphases within these treatment facilities supports health care that includes the practice of subtle energy interventions. With enhanced understandings from science and research, modern-day healers hold the intention of relieving constricted patterns in energy flow pathways and restoring the vital life force to its fullest levels.

Chapter Three
Gifts of the Human Energy System

When I talk about optimum health...I'm talking about ways of protecting, enhancing, or activating that internal potential to return to balance.
—Andrew Weil

The body is our hardware; our energy is the life source.
—Anodea Judith

The exercises in the first chapter are samples of methods used to restore balance to the human energy system. Touching specific energy points (acupoints) on the body while speaking self-affirming thoughts creates a sense of harmony. Other techniques relate to East Indian traditions, Chinese medicine, and other hybrids that current educators and therapists find effective in helping troubled adults and children. All come from an integrative framework that considers the whole person. The holistic, integrative approach addresses not only the physical body, the primary focus in Western medicine, but also our complex psychological, innately human dimensions. These dimensions include the inner emotional climate, thought patterns, spiritual understandings, and energy levels—all of which profoundly influence the body. Thus the exercises learned so far in this book are both psychological and energetic, or *psychoenergetic* exercises, within a holistic framework.

Energy concepts offer direct techniques for self-care and early intervention. They have become established as complementary to mainstream health care. Methods such as energy psychology, Therapeutic Touch, Healing Touch, Reiki, polarity therapy, Pranic

Healing, and psychoenergetic balancing are some of the best known. Yoga, tai chi, and qigong are also based on understanding of human energy flows.

Where did ideas to address human energies for healing originate? How do such ideas integrate with mainstream health care? How do we access their innate wisdoms? In this chapter, we'll explore one theoretical framework or metaphor behind the science and research discussed in the previous chapter.

A Short History of Healing Traditions

Throughout human history, people have sought ways to alleviate suffering from physical or emotional distress. Mothers comforted children by holding them, brushing the site of an injury, or "kissing away" pain. Healers from all cultures learned to sense areas of disturbance, depletion, or constriction surrounding the bodies of the ill. They then rebalanced the disturbed areas by clearing the congestion and restoring vitality.

The vital life force in humans has many names in worldwide traditions, including *qi* in Chinese medicine, *prana* in East Indian teachings, *agne* in Ayurvedic traditions, *spiritus* in Christian practices, *pneuma* in ancient Greek texts, and *subtle energy* or *bioenergy* in recent American and European scientific publications. Actively present in the well person, the vital life force is diminished by illness and wholly absent after physical death. While the physical body can still be seen after death, the essence of the person, the energy or vital life force, is gone.

In the past (and in many indigenous cultures in the present), energy-oriented healers were seen as wise elders who received insights by aligning with nature and accessing intuitive, internally guided perceptions. Over time in both the East and West, healing became defined as the art of restoring the patient's vital life force to its fullest potential. This essential energy then nourished physical, emotional, mental, and spiritual dimensions of the person.

Only in the past century has Western medical care become distanced from such natural processes. Specialized institutions were developed for administering chemical and/or surgical interventions. Emphasis shifted from the broad implications of whole-person *healing* to the more tightly defined idea of *cure*. Cure has come to mean the perceived cause of a problem and its bothersome symptoms are removed. As seen in present-day Western medical care, curing provides a decidedly narrow focus. By not fully addressing the reality of chronic, incurable diseases or lifelong conditions, it overlooks the interactive relationship between body, mind, spirit, and human vitality.

For the latter half of life, Western medicine's mechanistic options offer considerably less than is needed for optimal functioning. Mechanical approaches abound, such as: "If a knee is worn out, replace it" and "If your mood is low, take a pill." These perceptions do not honor our innate humanity. The body reacts dramatically to our emotions, thoughts, beliefs, and lifestyle patterns. Stress is cumulative, and so are habits of goodwill, altruism, energy rebalancing, and positive thinking—and all produce noticeable results over time.

The philosophy of curing does not satisfy the needs of today's health-conscious baby boomers. Statistics show that more than two-thirds of people over sixty seek out complementary, holistic therapies to augment current medical approaches with their perceived limitations.[1] These seekers want more: 1) They want to achieve high-level wellness and to live well into advancing years, and 2) they want to understand the cause of problems and possible methods of prevention.

Our own energy systems offer practical, hands-on approaches to access full-person healing. Documented results of energetic approaches include a number of healthful outcomes such as pain relief, reduced anxiety, increased attention and concentration, enhanced sense of well-being, and increased personal efficacy.[2] All these are highly desirable qualities for positive longevity.

The first bridge between Eastern holistic concepts and Western medicine occurred in 1970. Developed by nursing professor Dr. Dolores Krieger and her intuitive friend, Dora Kunz, Therapeutic Touch (TT) gave hospital personnel a direct method for augmenting medical care with a form of centered, energetic communication. Currently, practitioners of TT and other related biofield and chakra interventions number in the hundreds of thousands, and millions have experienced the relief these modalities offer. Research aimed at understanding the effects of these applications is ongoing.[3]

Since TT represents the first entrance of energetic modalities into Western health care, we'll begin by discussing the biofield and chakra theories supporting the practice. Later, we'll examine the meridians and their related acupoints. In both instances, we'll discover how unseen, nonmaterial energies can influence the whole person.

The Biofield and the Chakras

More than five thousand years ago, the wisdom traditions of India held that all living things consist of subtle energies. Sensitive healers could "see" the human energy field as an envelope or sheath surrounding the body. Metaphysical teachings called this sheath the *aura,* and twentieth-century scientists began to use the terms *biofield* or *energy field* to describe the subtle electromagnetic emanations that extend beyond the physical body.

Modern-day healers (nurses using TT, for example) use their hands to sense a person's energy field extending six to twenty-four inches from the body's surface and determine areas of distortion. Their perceptions may note asymmetry, thickness, thinness, congestion, depletion, roughness, coolness, heat, tension, vibration, or stickiness. If something is amiss, a portion or the entire field will differ from the field's normal, healthy, symmetrical fullness (see figures 3.1 and 3.2). Various techniques can be implemented to disperse congestion or blockage. This may happen quickly or more gradually, depending on the field's ability to respond.

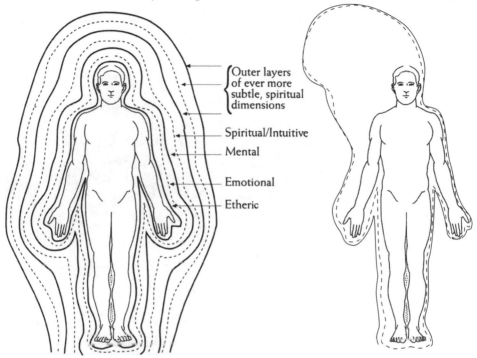

Outer layers of ever more subtle, spiritual dimensions

Spiritual/Intuitive

Mental

Emotional

Etheric

Figure 3.1: A healthy, symmetrical human energy field.

Figure 3.2: An unhealthy, asymmetrical energy field.

Other components of subtle energies described in yogic traditions are energy centers which relate to the body and biofield. Because they resemble spinning vortices of subtle energy, the term *chakra* (the Sanskrit word for wheel or vortex) is most commonly used. The seven major chakras align with the human spine from the base of the tailbone to the crown of the head and interpenetrate the layers of the biofield (see figure 3.3).

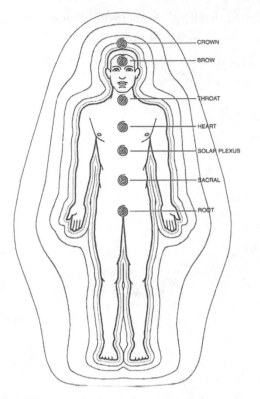

Figure 3.3: The seven major chakras in the human energy field.

A balanced, healthy person also has small chakras between the bones at every joint that vibrate in harmony with the whole biofield. Chakras relate to endocrine gland flows that send chemical and hormonal messages throughout the body. They also have distinctive psychological meanings that correspond to progressive developmental stages of human life.[4]

Most people readily sense the locations of the chakras, whether they are aware of it or not. Descriptions such as "I have a gut feeling," "I feel like the bottom is dropping out," "I have a frog in my throat," and "My heart is bursting with joy" capture actual physical sensations of chakra energy. Sensed distortions in the energy flow of one or more chakras can help identify somatic and psychological issues. Knowledge of the chakras increases our sensitivity to internal states that we might otherwise tend to ignore. Because they support intuitive knowledge and personal awareness, the chakras are best understood as centers of consciousness.

The Root or Base Chakra

The chakra sequence extends from the most basic survival and safety mechanisms, reflected in quick adrenal stress responses, to the more ethereal work of the pituitary gland in regulating body metabolisms and the pineal gland in signaling essential biorhythms. In a similar vein, psychological needs such as a basic security must be met before we can move to higher levels of insight, compassion, and purpose for our lives. Each stage of life builds on previous ones as we allow full potentials to flourish.

The functions of the root chakra remind us to stand firmly, feeling our connection to the earth and gift of life. A willingness to trust and explore new ways of being requires strong grounding lest one become distracted by fear or mistrust. Trusting life and its many lessons requires investing time and money in seeking help when needed. The will to live and find joy are signs of optimal functioning of this chakra. The natural capacity to dance and move is its physical expression.

Some life-affirming thoughts for the root chakra are:

- I feel my energy.
- I'm glad to be alive.
- I am safe and secure.
- Beyond my present distractions, the universe is basically friendly.
- I meet each challenge with curiosity, trusting my path.

The color red is often associated with this center. Its vibrational patterns, sensed by intuitive persons, were confirmed by studies with experienced meditators who, when focusing on the root chakra, also showed activation of the color red in the frequency spectrum.[5] If you wish to increase your vitality and basic life force, wear or surround yourself with bright red materials.

The sound that most exemplifies this center is drumming. The recent rise in popular drumming circles may represent our society's need to reconnect with the root chakra's grounding energies.

The Sacral Chakra

Below the navel and at the sacrum (the flat bony triangle at the lower back) lies the sacral center. Bodily functions of this area are associated with sexuality as well as assimilation and absorption of nutrients in the large intestines. Psychologically speaking, this chakra is associated with emotional expression and choosing appropriate relationships. It also reminds us to let go of what does not fit, just like the large intestine releases surplus materials. When our feelings are numbed, we may also lose track of our pelvic region and its important releasing functions. Optimal function is accompanied by easy, positive relationships with others, freedom from addictions, and ability to integrate new ideas.

Affirmations for the sacral chakra are:

- I accept myself as a feeling person.
- I give myself permission to feel.
- I value and respect my feelings.
- I choose what is valuable to me and to release what does ot fit.
- I choose the relationships that are right for me.

The color orange is most frequently associated with this center. In Buddhist traditions, orange robes worn by monks signify their mastery of the emotional dimension. The emotionally calming sound of the flute is most related to the sacral chakra.

The Solar Plexus

The solar plexus, located at the base of the sternum and a corresponding place on the back, is the central place of sensing one's personal power. Physical conditions such as stomach ulcers, hypo- or hyperglycemia, and digestive disturbances relate to energetic blockage in this chakra. Emotionally, this center relates to clear thinking and taking charge of one's life. People with powerful ego demands and needs to dominate present an overabundance of *qi* in this center. Self-effacing, passive persons exhibit diminished, even depleted solar plexus energy. Both are distortions. Healthy manifestations of this chakra are ability to think clearly and effectively assert oneself. The center represents the will to think and is also associated with staying power, that is, the ability to start a project, implement it, and bring it to completion.

Affirmations for the solar plexus are:

- I sense and appreciate my inner power.

- I can think clearly.

- I can assert myself appropriately when needed.

- I feel my strengths and respect the strengths of others.

- I am neither too weak nor too strong in my communications with others.

The color yellow is the vibrational frequency of this center. Sweet-sounding stringed instruments are its musical essence.

Exercise 3.1 Strengthening the Lower Three Chakras

The lower three chakras are connected to our primary needs: the will to live, to feel, and to think. As we clear obstructions out of each center, we open ourselves to the power of higher wisdoms.

1. Allow yourself to stand or sit while consciously imaging your connection to the earth.

2. Hold your hands over the perineal area while gently brushing out any negative thoughts about your life at the moment.

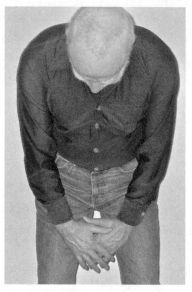

Hold your hands over the perineal area to
begin strengthening the lower chakras.

3. Then bring in positive affirmations about your will to live as fully as possible. Contracting the sphincter muscles gives a sense of the physical location of this center. You may also add a spin to the right or imagine it. Imagine the color red and add the sound of drumming if desired.

4. Next, hold your hands over the sacral area below the navel and gently brush out any obstructions to full permission to connect with your feelings.

5. Bring in positive affirmations about being connected to your emotions and trusting them to serve as antennae. Imagine the color orange and hear the gentle sound of a flute.

6. Next, hold your hands over the solar plexus and gently brush out any hindrances to thinking clearly and speaking up when needed.

7. Bring in positive affirmations about your abilities to commu-
    nicate effectively. See the color yellow and hear the sounds of
    strings.

8. To complete the exercise, allow yourself to see all three centers
    supporting you like the strong foundations of a well-designed
    building. Feel the energy of your stable, solid intentions. Take
    a deep breath and affirm your aliveness with the ability to feel
    and think.

The Heart Chakra

As we move to the higher chakras, we note a shift to heart-cen-
tered caring and more subtle dimensions. Compassionate insight and
caring for others flows from the support of the lower centers and
the activation of the heart. The lower centers address physical, emotional, and mental energies. The heart center touches the soul and is
associated with the will to love and forgive.

Located at the center of the chest, the heart center qualities are
harmony, appreciation, accepting love, and forgiving ourselves as well
as others.

Affirmations for the heart chakra are:

• I now give and receive unconditional love.

• The more I can forgive myself, the more I can forgive others.

• As I care for myself, I am able to give care to others.

• As I show appreciation for myself, others are more able to appreciate themselves.

Healthy heart center energy sends empowering messages to the
immune system via the thymus gland. It also nurtures blood circu-
lation and the respiratory system. Since heart, lung, and immune
system disorders are leading causes of premature death, it is apparent
our present world suffers greatly from heart center dysfunctions.

When psychological work is done to release grudges and resentments and to forgive others, the heart chakra energy expands and causes all our immune functions to become more active. The associated color is life-giving green. The ringing, expanding vibration of a large bell is the heart's essential sound.

The Throat Chakra

The throat center is located at the neck, both front and back, and relates to creative self-expression. Also, more subtle perceptions of senses begin here. Optimal functions are noted in speaking with a strong voice, trusting one's inner truth, and strong self-esteem. The capabilities of this chakra allow for expression of our talents, knowledge, and understanding as we explore enhanced longevity.

Affirmations for the throat chakra are:

- I enjoy expressing who I am.
- I speak my truth.
- I allow others to express their truths.
- I am curious about new things.
- I enjoy my innate intuition.

The colors turquoise or light blue express the vibration of this center. The sound of wind rushing through trees is the related sound.

The Brow Chakra

The brow center was often called the "third eye" in ancient texts. Associated with deep compassion flowing from the caring heart, it is modified by intuitive perceptions and holds the ability to put oneself in another's place, as native American wisdom counsels, "to walk a mile in another's shoes." It is a center of wisdom. With the support of the lower centers, intuitive knowing becomes compassionate wisdom. Distortions are making judgments without compassion or using intuition to exert control over others.

Affirmations for the brow chakra are:

- I view things with insight.

- I reach out to others with compassion and wisdom.

- I release prejudices and judgments.

- I seek the resources I need to be most effective in helping others.

The color of deep indigo blue captures the vibrational signature of this center. The sound is one of waves crashing on a beach.

The Crown Chakra

The crown center is seen as the connection of inner wisdom to the oneness of the universe. It is the center of soul-consciousness and spirituality. Spirituality emerging with activation of this center is not limited to a particular religion. Rather, it follows the quest for meaning in life and honors the perception of forces much greater, and more trustworthy, than the individual ego. Statistics bear out that people with spiritual faith live longer and handle stress more equitably.[6]

Affirmations for the crown chakra are:

- I open to expanded consciousness.

- I seek out higher wisdom.

- I appreciate the power behind the wonders of nature.

- I trust that there is a positive plan for my life.

Associated colors are the entire rainbow but especially lavender, gold, and silver vibrations. The sound is that of a full orchestra or a choir singing in full voice.

Exercise 3.2 Through the Decades with the Chakras

With the support of the lower three centers (and active use of exercise 3.1), you can now focus on the higher chakras with their affirmations, colors, and sounds. As you are ready, repeat the affirmations you have selected for each center until they become natural for you.

Some believe the chakra sequence corresponds roughly to life decades with their developmental tasks toward deepening wisdom. Developmental psychologist Erik Erikson views the culmination of personal growth as mature development of one's generativity and integrity. The alternatives to personality expansion in later life are stagnation and despair.[7] This exercise asks you to examine your experiences with the centers of consciousness in each of your life stages.

1. Seated comfortably, clear out any tension with a few deep relaxation breaths.

2. As you think about the first decade of your life, recall how trust in walking, talking, and being alive was nurtured. If it was not, due to neglect or abuse, release the distress and bring in root chakra affirmations.

3. Think about the teenage years of raging sex hormones with the roller coaster of feelings you had. Recall how you resolved those issues and which people supported you unconditionally. Affirm your present abilities to be aware of emotions and to seek out resources you need to handle strong emotions.

4. Think of your early twenties, career choices, selecting a partner, and how you began taking charge of your life. Note the ways you made choices and how you thought things through.

5. Note your increasing caring for others in your thirties, your growing relationships with family members and community. Remember how true caring was expressed. Did life become better with increased self-acceptance and self-care?

6. Notice the shift to more creativity in your forties or fifties. Alternately, be aware how you may have held yourself back. Did you have a midlife slump? Or did you move forward with hope and enthusiasm into the second half of life?

7. Give attention to the times an intuitive awareness came to you. Did you heed or ignore it? Would you like to expand your compassion and insight?

8. Move your attention to the crown and ask what beliefs most support you. Do you perceive yourself as an evolving spiritual being? Have you cut off your sense of connection to the wonders of nature? What in your life is of greater importance and value than yourself?

9. Jot down your thoughts from this exercise, noting which chakras are more naturally developed in you and which ones you may wish to learn more about.

We can see richness of the chakras for personal development at any age. Only our youth-focused culture suggests that people stop growing emotionally, mentally, and spiritually at midlife. Each center has unique gifts as we choose to develop and mature. All centers are needed in order to become fully alive in the second half of life.

The Meridians and Related Acupoints

More than five thousand years ago, Chinese civilization explored subtle human energies in a slightly different way. Similar to yoga traditions, they believed all living things were imbued with vital life force they called *qi*. They "saw" or sensed the flow of *qi* in the form of pathways that interpenetrated different organs of the body. The flow pathways, called *meridians,* became associated with a body organ and were given names such as the lung meridian, or small intestine meridian. The name of the meridian, however, is not limited to the organ since each meridian travels through the entire body. Like the chakras, meridians also impact both physical and psychological functions throughout the whole human energy system.[8] (See figure 3.4.)

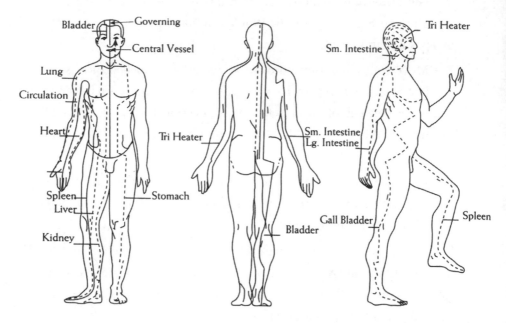

Figure 3.4: Meridians, or energy pathways, used in Chinese medicine.

The meridians are electromagnetic in nature.[9] Numerous specific points along each meridian, called *acupoints*, function as relay stations to boost very slight currents. As presently understood, acupoints are akin to relays used in electrical wiring circuits. Stimulation of acupoints by fine needles, applying heat, or gentle tapping was fully integrated into Chinese medicine. The effects of acupoint stimulation are relief of pain, increased sense of well-being, and enhanced wound healing. The most dramatic use of acupoint stimulation is its deep anesthetic effects during surgical procedures. Only one or two needles skillfully placed are needed to "anesthetize" the patient. Acupuncture practitioners typically learn over a thousand acupoints and receive years of training to achieve their remarkable results.

Yet despite its beneficial effects, acupuncture was not approved by the American Medical Association until 1997 and then only for limited use.[10] Conditions approved for acupuncture include chronic pain, side effects of chemotherapy, and headaches.

In the 1980s, psychologist Roger Callahan found that tapping or holding specific acupoints (no needles!) could bring about emotional relief. He was able to relieve anxiety and treat intense phobias with the method he developed, called Thought Field Therapy (TFT), in an amazingly short period of time. Since then, a number of practices have emerged using a variety of acupoint sequences. One of the best known is Emotional Freedom Techniques (EFT), an offshoot of Callahan's work developed by Gary Craig.[11] To date, psychologist Fred Gallo has written the greatest number of books about the fascinating technologies that he named "energy psychology."[12] Numerous other studies, articles, and books about energy psychology, which includes EFT, TFT, and other therapies, have been published in the last decade.

The most frequently used acupoints for the many meridian therapies are fourteen points along the identified fourteen major meridians (see figure 3.5). These can be stimulated to relieve anxiety, enhance self-confidence, and bring about rapid change in emotional states. They are effective tools for change, as we will learn.

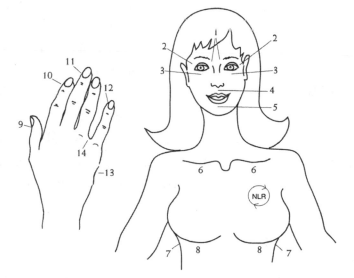

Figure 3.5: The fourteen acupoints used in Thought Field Therapy (TFT).

Comprehensive Energy Therapies

Some people find that meridian work releases issues quickly; others prefer the more in-depth structure of working with the chakras. All energy approaches seem to restore inner balance by reminding us of our innate wellness.

The Association for Comprehensive Energy Psychology, founded in 1999, exists to validate and extend the applications of a wide variety of energy concepts to psychotherapy. Membership in ACEP includes more than a thousand counselors, social workers, psychologists, psychiatrists, nurses, addictions specialists, acupuncturists, and a host of related health-care workers and interested laypersons, including representatives from twenty-seven countries. ACEP honors the paths utilizing meridians, biofield/chakra networks, and related therapies. Numerous conferences and workshops taught nationally and internationally support personal growth and collegial exchange.[13]

****

Healing ourselves is a lifelong commitment of ongoing psychological development, self-understanding, and finding our life's goals. The energy tools discussed here give access to a large treasure trove of self-help tools to enhance quality of life at any age. They may also help to prevent illness or ameliorate the effects of disease and pain by providing easily accessible tools for self-care. Regularly maintaining energetic balance is a vital resource for joyous living.

In the rest of this book, you will discover how aspects of your energy system can help you deal with day-to-day difficulties, install more desirable thought patterns, and move into your full creative potential.

Part II:

Applications of
Energy Psychology Concepts
in Daily Life

Chapter Four
Make Sure Your System is "On"

As long as we can still be inspired, we know we are alive,
refusing to join the procession of the living dead.
—Angeles Arrien

Choosing Well-Being or Acedia

Although it's quite easy to feel vital and alive in the first half of life, sustaining and conserving vitality in the second half of life is generally more challenging. Optimal aging is connected with strong intention and genuine dedication to the art of well-being. Stagnation, despair, boredom, loneliness, and indifference indicate blocks to the flow of generative energy, the vital life force. These experiences are called *acedia,* from the Greek work *akedos,* meaning "not caring" or "sour." Acedia weakens the soul over time with lack of passion, dissipation of energy, misdirected quests for recognition, or self-imposed isolation. Such psychological death is by far a much greater concern than physical death for the nation's aging population.

Aliveness after midlife, as opposed to a living psychological death, is supported and cultivated by establishing energetic balance from within. We begin by focusing on the biofield, which extends through and beyond the physical body and can be measured in medicine with the technology of SQUID (superconducting quantum interference device). As patterns of disruption from *qi* continue, cellular messaging is disturbed as well and the body weakens. As seen in the previous chapter, the body's immune system translates thoughts into intercellular messages. Richard Gerber, MD, author of *Vibrational Medicine,* writes: "When the body is in a healthy energetic vibrational mode, a small innoculum of virus is easily discharged from the body. In an individual who is energetically imbalanced and thus immunologically weakened, this same viral exposure may allow a serious systemic viral illness to occur."[1]

Lifelong patterns of energetic disturbance are frequently seen in counseling settings. Clients report difficulty concentrating, inability to accomplish goals, becoming easily confused, having trouble with directions, or feeling basically unhappy with themselves. They may show a history of going to many counselors without obtaining relief. Since these symptoms point to psychological as well as energetic components, we call such disturbances a form of *psychoenergetic imbalance.*

Psychoenergetic imbalance is a pervasive human distress. It can, if ignored, lead to more serious physical or emotional distortions. There are many labels from different disciplines (nursing, chiropractic, psychotherapy, naturopathic practices, and more) to describe the sense of disconnection and inner shakiness felt after a traumatic incident. In addition to the diagnostic term of "energy field disturbance," psychoenergetic imbalance, neurological disorganization, systemic nonpolarization, or "being switched" are frequently used. Whatever the label, something is amiss and accompanied by a vague sense of discomfort. The internal effect is very real, yet nothing can be consistently documented from an objective, medical point of view.

We may all be at risk for "energy field disturbance" because of the current political climate. Anxiety, irritability, and a nonspecific sense of fear have risen remarkably since the 9/11 terrorist attacks and heighten with every news alert. Skillful means are needed to ensure that we maintain a sense of objectivity and inner peace despite the media's escalating doomsday prophecies.

Fear-based thinking is an early warning signal of energetic distur- bance. The disturbances may later develop into physical or emotional disruptions. In the beginning, the sensitive subtle energy body may just register something to be a bit "off." By addressing the dishar- mony, we can treat imbalance before it becomes concretized into physical or psychological symptoms. As we might guess, the symp- toms of acedia tend to increase over time unless conscious effort is made to overcome them.

Treating the Effects of Bad News

As part of an integrative approach, we can relieve system-wide energetic disturbance. In a crisis or after trauma, it is crucial for people to seek relief as soon as possible. Otherwise, bad news may be passively absorbed and hinder reconnecting with innate wholeness. The simplest methods are usually best because they are most easily remembered.

Practitioners of Therapeutic Touch share this wisdom. They do simple energetic maneuvers called "unruffling."[2] This is a purpose- ful sweeping, clearing, or smoothing of the biofield. Practitioners also use this technique in emergency room triage settings and on themselves during a crisis. Similarly, meridian therapy practitioners remember to rub the two acupoints that are part of the central meridian flow vessels—under the nose, and under the lip—as a treatment for shock. This technique can be expanded into the more extensive interventions described in the exercises to follow.

Although there are hundreds of methods for rebalancing the human energy system, the ones I offer here are a sampling of possible approaches. The regular practice of centering as presented in the fol- lowing exercise has been shown to improve immune system function and increase the flow of antiaging hormones.[3] When a troublesome event is having an impact on your life or whenever you feel stressed, try using one of these exercises or several in combination.

Exercise 4.1 Central Alignment[4]

1. Standing or sitting comfortably, visualize a vibrant line of energy that flows through the center of your body in relation to your head and spine. See the connection from the base of your spine and down through your feet to the very core of the earth.

2. Place your hands on the gravitational center of the body, which is an inch or so below the navel. You will always move in balanced ways when your focus is on this *hara* area, a yoga point for physical focusing and the gravitational center of the body. Visualize the connection between your *hara* and the earth's core.

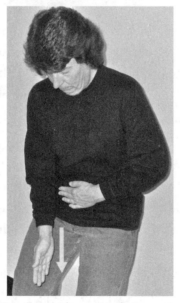

Visualize the hara-Earth connection.

3. Let your awareness shift as you move one hand to the upper mid-chest, halfway between the belly button and the spurasternal notch, while keeping the other hand on the *hara*. The upper mid-chest is considered the "soul seat," the area where we begin to experience our sense of personal purpose and meaning. Allow

the connection between the two hands to strengthen while breathing fully. Continue to feel your grounding connection to the earth.

4. While still keeping one hand on the *hara,* move the other hand from the mid-chest to above the crown of your head. Then stretch this hand upward toward your favorite celestial star. Sense the alignment between all parts of your unique energy line: your cosmic star, soul seat, *hara,* and connection to the earth.

Feel the alignment between your celestial star and the hara.

5. Allow a sense of color or a sound to assist your image of this central line. (As some people do this exercise, they "see" vibrant images of the spiral double helix, the structural arrangement of DNA molecule strands.)

6. Gently return to full awareness, letting your hands drop and noting changes in your body and mind. Practice walking around the room with your sense of inner alignment. Imagine walking with the strength of this central alignment into a difficult situation in your community or at home. Notice your sense of increased confidence.

Exercise 4.2 Chakra Rotation

This exercise utilizes the major energy vortices, or chakras, which relate to the body from the base of the spine to the top of the head. Bringing conscious awareness to each center while spinning the body gently brings increased vitality to the entire energy system.

1. While standing comfortably, allow yourself to center and feel grounded to the earth. Begin by spreading your hands on your thighs, bending your knees, sensing the connection to the earth through your hands and feet.

2. Sense the inflow of your life force from nature and the sun into your heart center. Hold both hands over the heart center as you focus there with a sense of gratitude and thanksgiving.

With hands on heart, focus on gratitude.

3. Bring the energy of gratitude from the heart center to the root chakra area at the base of the spine, while affirming your joy at being alive in the physical body. If desired, add vigorous clockwise rotations with your hips as you would if you were spinning a hula hoop.

4. Next, allow *qi* to flow from your hands to the sacral center, just below the navel in the front and at the small of the back. Affirm your ability to select and choose the nutrients, people, and situations that are right for you. Continue the rotations with your hips while focusing your attention on the sacral area.

5. Bring your awareness and your hands to the solar plexus with its strengths for taking charge, thinking clearly, and communicating effectively. Add a slight spin or rotation with your body while feeling your assertiveness.

6. Let *qi* now flow freely from your hands to the heart center. Enjoy a sense of acceptance and forgiveness. Imagine reaching out to your loved ones and then bringing in their caring with large arm movements.

7. Bring your hands over the throat area, front and back, while sensing support from the universe for your creativity. Allow your voice to make a sound, finding the tone that is pleasing to you. Try all five vowels with this tone; play with various sounds; make up rhymes or hum a tune.

8. Allow the hands to rest over the brow area while affirming your ability to develop higher sense perception and to use insight with compassion.

9. Bring the hands to the crown while feeling the inflow of *qi* from the universe. Sense the connection with infinite peace, love, and wisdom for your life with its special gifts and sense of purpose.

10. Let your whole being continue to resonate with a sense of peace and enhanced alertness, feeling the joy of being alive throughout your energy system. Notice changes in your body and mind before going on to your next task.

Exercise 4.3 The Zip Up

This exercise traces the pathway of one of the midline meridians, known as the central or conception (idea-generating) vessel. Tracing each single meridian is another effective way to bring more *qi* into the body.

1. While standing or sitting comfortably, cup the palms of your hands together over the pubic bone and set your intent on energizing yourself. Take a deep breath and release it fully.

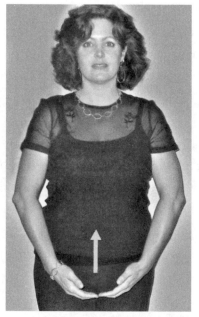

In the Zip Up, cup your hands over the pubic bone.

2. Then, while inhaling, bring the hands slowly up along the midline until you come to the lower lip. Lock in the sense of increased *qi* with a slight swirl at each side of the lower lip acupoint. Let the hands drop and simultaneously release the breath fully.

3. Repeat this several more times until you feel a surge of confidence and self-esteem within you. Repeat the whole process as often as needed to give yourself an energetic boost.

Exercise 4.4 The Crossover Correction

This exercise, adapted from Educational Kinesiology,[5] includes a yoga posture, and permits integration of the right and left hemispheres of the brain, the two central meridians, and the breath. It crosses as many midline pathways as possible. I have found it extremely helpful in treating tiredness, confusion, and anxiety—the symptoms of energetic imbalance that most people experience daily.

1. Take a deep breath and release it fully. Cross the left ankle over the right and make sure your body is comfortable while you are sitting, lying down, or standing.

2. Bring your hands in front of you with the backs of the hands facing each other and the thumbs pointing down. Cross the right hand over the left and then bring both together toward you while inverting the clasped hands so the thumbs face away from you.

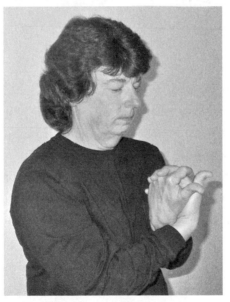

The Crossover Correction.

3. Breathe easily while you let the tongue touch the roof of the mouth as you inhale. As you exhale, let the tongue drop down to the floor of the mouth.

4. Hold this posture for several minutes until you feel a sense of inner calm and peace. Release any tension with each out-breath, and let the in-breath bring a sense of peacefulness. If you wish, add a peaceful sound or warming color.

5. Notice any changes in your body and mind after doing this exercise.

Exercise 4.5 Anchoring a Self-Affirming Mantra

One of the most global energetic disturbances is low self-esteem. This can be addressed with a *mantra* (a repeated, self-affirming, positive statement) while gently rubbing a neurolymphatic reflex point. One of these points is the tender spot located on the left side of the upper mid-chest, about where Americans place their right hand for the Pledge of Allegiance. Touching this point allows the statement and its meaning to be felt in the body, as if "anchored" to your physical reality.

1. While rubbing the tender spot toward the left shoulder in small circles, repeat at least three times, "I deeply and profoundly accept myself with all my faults, problems, and limitations."

2. Other words can be used, but it is important for the intent to be clear: deep self-acceptance that exceeds current issues and distractions. Some people feel greater comfort with a more positively worded affirmation, such as: "I deeply and profoundly accept myself with all my gifts, talents, and ability to love." (Again, repeat at least three times while rubbing the tender spot.)

These affirmations help to establish a sense of hope and self-acceptance. Many who add the "pledge spot" to their favorite affirmation report a calming, comforting effect.

Exercise 4.6 The Belly-Button Connection

This exercise, adapted from Educational Kinesiology,[6] stimulates several meridian points to help restore systemic balance: under the nose for the governing vessel; under the lip for the central vessel;

at the collarbone for the kidney meridian; and at the base of the tailbone for the starting point of the governing vessel. In addition, because it uses the belly button as a connecting point, it is familiar, comforting, and fun. Touching the fingertips to each other at the end gives closure to the exercise and integrates the right and left brain hemispheres.

1. While sitting or standing, take a deep breath, release it fully, and set your intention of allowing your system to establish balance.

2. Place one hand on the belly button while moving the other hand to touch the points under the nose and under the lip. Rub lightly for ten to fifteen seconds to stimulate each point and to set your *vertical alignment* for integration of the upper and lower parts of the body.

Setting the vertical alignment in the Belly-Button Connection.

3. While keeping the hand on the belly button, move the other hand to the two collarbone points and rub lightly to set your *horizontal alignment* for balance between the right and left sides of the body.

4. Still keeping the hand on the belly button, move your other hand to the end of the tailbone, rubbing lightly to set *alignment between the front and back* of your body.

5. Switch by placing your other hand on the belly button and repeat steps 2 through 4.

6. Continuing to breathe fully, bring your fingertips together and hold for a few minutes to feel the integration of your body, mind, and spirit.

****

Restoring balance in the body's energy field is readily available with some of the exercises suggested here. Use them daily or as often as needed to feel your vitality and aliveness. A simple clue is to start with the exercise that seems easiest to remember or the one that is the most fun. Then add another just for good measure.

Our thoughts and reactions constantly affect our subtle energies. The beliefs and habit patterns that shape our biography also become our biology. In the next two chapters, we will explore the impact of thinking patterns, responses to life's challenges, and tools for personal empowerment.

Chapter Five
Revising Belief Habit Trails

What we believe is the most powerful option of all.
—Norman Cousins

Managing day-to-day stresses by releasing and rebalancing allows a closer look at core beliefs about aging. Most dysfunctional thinking patterns are carried without notice. They are like the "blind spots" when driving a car.

Examples of dysfunctional belief patterns are: "Aging will be difficult," "Memory gets worse with age," "Retirement is a time of rest and withdrawal from life," and "Seniors need to rest and sit back." Ideas about aging and retirement can be as varied as we choose, but over time, they impact thinking, behavior, and even cellular structures and DNA patterning.

Gordon believed he was losing his mind after his wife died. He could not remember where he had placed important documents and often found himself standing still on the way to look for something, having forgotten what it was. His fears escalated when friends tried to cheer him by saying "Oh, you're just having another senior moment." Gordon began thinking he was on his way to dementia, although frequent loss of concentration is quite commonly experienced in grieving. After understanding this pattern from a therapist, he learned to treat his beliefs about his mind in the kindly way offered by energy psychology and explained in this chapter.

Rather than worrying about possible memory loss, we can affirm ways to enhance our thinking prowess with novelty and creativity. There are many ways to update limiting beliefs and maintain positive mindsets. At the same time, we can acknowledge it's sometimes good to forget accumulated trivia.

In this chapter we learn how to release and transform limiting mindsets into more functional, desirable, and empowering beliefs. We will explore:

- The reality of limiting mindsets

- Identifying limiting beliefs and core patterns

- Identifying desired, empowering beliefs

- Strategies for releasing limiting patterns from the meridian acupoints and the chakras

- Strategies for installing empowering, desirable beliefs through the acupoints and the chakras

- Finding positive intention within us to forgive the past and trust new discoveries.

Redirecting limiting patterns toward effective behavioral styles can be surprisingly easy with the psychoenergetic approaches proposed here. Working with the chakras, the biofield, and the meridian acupoints—the major aspects of the human vibrational matrix—gives delightful resources for daily self-care and for transforming habitual thinking patterns into new resources and ideas.

Limiting Mindsets... Who, Me?

Several central beliefs, sometimes called a core belief complex, can inform the whole personality structure. Examples are: "I don't like myself," "I am confused," "I am betrayed by my family," "I am powerless and helpless in the current political world," "I'm a failure, "I have nothing left to live for," "I am a victim," and "The world is dangerous." Such broad generalizations help to spawn a large cadre of negative thinking patterns and a worldview of mistrust and unhappiness. Like a magnet, they attract ever more limiting beliefs.

Limiting mindsets about aging abound in today's culture. They can undermine and erode self-esteem in subtle ways. Think of the times someone may have ignored you because of your hair color or wrinkles. Perhaps, you were seated in a restaurant corner to be out of sight or a waitress used a patronizing voice with you. Think of times someone honked at you because you drove more slowly than others for safety. Elders can be marginalized in many ways. But even more damaging than the actions of others are the many ways our own beliefs limit and constrict thinking. Ongoing negativity attacks the very essence of the personality.

I recently met a man who said "No!" to every suggestion made by his wife or friends. The pattern became so automatic, it often happened even before anyone else could even complete a sentence or request. His demeanor became gruff, rigid, and unresponsive to every kindness around him. Barely into his seventies, this man became a distorted figure of the lively, successful person he used to be. One might conclude that, instead of evolving as a human being, he had "devolved" to a constricting imprisonment of his being.

Like the person who wants to lose weight but does not change eating habits, limiting mindsets create the opposite of a person's intentions. People may sabotage themselves just when they most need to be mindful and alert. Psychoanalytic theory calls counter-intentions the work of the unconscious mind and foresees years of therapy to correct such basic patterns. The energy system model perceives unconsciously held beliefs as reversals or constrictions. Hence these psychoenergetic reversals (also known as objections to succeeding) can readily be addressed by activating the innate wisdom of the energy system.

Matt's Story: Performance Terror

Since music is meant to be shared, issues around public performance inevitably surface in my work with musicians. When I ask performers to list their most absurd or limiting beliefs, core issues about self-esteem and self-confidence surface quickly. Perceptions from inferred childhood trauma become internalized because they are given by powerful adults long before the person developed adequate defenses or coping mechanisms. These perceived notions dramatically shape performers' public abilities in later life.

I asked retired physician Matt to itemize reasons for his negative thoughts about playing his beloved ragtime piano tunes in public. He replied: "If I perform, I might make a mistake...If I make a mistake, I will be wrong...I'm not good enough...If I'm wrong, it means I'm not a good doctor...If I'm wrong, I will be a poor role model for my grandchildren...If I'm wrong, everyone in the family will laugh at me." As his list lengthened, I could see him accessing sheer terror. The core issues touched by this simple exercise were much larger than being a retired physician and grandfather but led him to issues from a childhood family structure of intimidation and embarrassment.

Matt sensed the terror of public performance in all three of his lower chakras related to safety, permission to feel, and permission to think. I asked him to release the most powerful old belief from each of the three energy centers with a vigorous spin with the hands to the right (counterclockwise). He chose "My family (of origin) will laugh at me" as the most damaging core issue. He then released it with vigorous expulsive sounds from each chakra. As he let go of the judging family's image, Matt spontaneously saw them smiling and cheering him on in a more kindly fashion.

I then asked which new affirmation would be helpful to Matt in overcoming the old belief. Within a moment, he had it: "Even if I make a mistake, my friends still love me." He anchored the new belief into his body by holding his hands over each chakra from the root up while stating it and giving each chakra a clockwise spin.

Matt's self-confidence grew as he released the old fear of public embarrassment. Within this new climate of self-acceptance, he began to thrive as a congenial musician at senior center social events.

Dumping Limiting Mindsets

Working with the chakras is one way of using movement to release embedded patterns and bring in new possibilities. An alternate method for releasing limiting beliefs is to use the fourteen acupoints of the meridian system (following the fourteen acupoints given in figure 3.5). Once you identify a limiting belief, you can state, "I now release_____," while either holding or tapping lightly at each acupoint, starting at the eyebrows.

Another approach is to rub the tender spot on the upper mid-chest while repeatedly affirming your strengths. For example, "Even if I make a mistake, I deeply and profoundly accept myself." Possibly, the phrase "I deeply and profoundly forgive myself for having made a mistake" would be more effective for someone prone to guilt feelings. In either case, your intent is to overcome negative beliefs about making mistakes or being wrong and to widen your perspective.

The human creative process requires us to look at mistakes and then move forward with insights we have gained. People who want to live fully accept the reality of repeated risking and reorganizing on a daily basis: Artists may paint twenty pictures before selecting one they value enough to display; musicians practice over and over to perform and share with audiences; photographers shoot hundreds of pictures to find the right angle; and good architects design and redesign hundreds of times until they master the discipline and develop their own style.

Identifying and releasing the powerful influence of limiting beliefs is half of the work. Installing new, more functional patterns is the other half. We must let go of disturbances or constrictions before new ideas, balance, or harmony can fill their place. Once distress has been cleared out, the creative human mind has a magical capacity to attract what it wishes and make it real with a single word, phrase, or image.

Jenny's Story:
Out-of-Date Patterns Traded In for New Thoughts

Like many people, Jenny had self-doubts about speaking in front of others. Yet, as a retired public accountant, she felt she had something to share with her elder community about financial planning. We spent a long time identifying her dysfunctional beliefs regarding public speaking. During the session, she remembered a fifth grade teacher who made fun of her for mumbling, and many tears came forth.

When I suggested each limiting belief had a more empowering counterpart, things began to brighten. We came up with a list similar to the one given in table 5.1. The column on the left listed limiting beliefs and the right-hand column stated the desired possibilities.

You could make a similar list. Dysfunctional beliefs you hold about yourself or a related issue go on one side while contrasting, opposite statements go on the other. This will provide a sense of new possibilities for accessing positive, empowering thoughts. Be gentle with yourself when considering changes to your established thinking patterns; it takes courage and resilience to look objectively at oneself. Instead of exclaiming "What a lousy person I am for having so many crummy thoughts!" honor yourself with a caring statement such as "I have baggage from the past, but I also have the courage to make changes." By focusing on empowering patterns, you engender a sense of hope and friendliness toward your own being.

Table 5.1 Sample of Limiting Beliefs about Public Speaking and Desired New Beliefs

Limiting Belief	Desired New Belief
If I show who I really am, I will be criticized.	If I show who I really am, I may be criticized or praised.
If I express myself, it will be dangerous.	When I express myself, I can plan for my safety. I can feel good about myself in all settings.
When I express myself, I will be in danger.	When I express myself, I can be safe. I create my safety.
If listeners do not like what I say, it's my fault.	If listeners do not like what I say, it's their choice.
I am afraid of ridicule.	I can deal with ridicule. I don't have to like it.
If I express myself, I will be misunderstood.	If I express myself, I can learn to be understood. Some will understand and some will not; it's their choice.
If a teacher does not like my speech, I will never give another. (She'll be sorry!)	If any teacher does not like my speech, it will be her choice. I can give as many speeches as I choose.
I am embarrassed to speak about myself.	I can learn much if I speak about myself.
I dislike making mistakes.	I can learn from my mistakes. Not learning from my mistakes would be a major error.

Belief-Changing Strategies

The following exercises further clarify possible approaches for identifying and releasing old patterns and installing more desirable and functional beliefs. Establishing psychoenergetic balance through centering practices (you can use one or two exercises from the previous chapter) is helpful before engaging in more specific work such as this.

Exercise 5.1 Releasing Limiting Beliefs through the Chakras

1. While standing or sitting comfortably, think of a limiting belief you have regarding your creativity or another identified issue. Notice where in your body you feel it most.

2. Bring your hands to this area while thinking of all related beliefs or identified memories you may be holding there. Consider anything that might be keeping you from letting go of these limiting mindsets.

3. With your hands over the affected area, spin your hands counterclockwise to the right to sweep out the pattern you wish to release. Stating the old belief out loud while using expressive, expulsive sounds and movements will further enhance this work.

Releasing limited beliefs through the chakras.

4. Go through all of the chakras from top to bottom in a similar fashion. When you complete this sequence, punctuate it with an exultation, such as "Yeah!" "Wow!" "Hallelujah!"

5. Notice any images or thoughts that come to you now. When you have done this, you will be ready to bring in new, more desirable beliefs.

Exercise 5.2 Installing Desirable Beliefs through the Chakras

1. Think of an empowering belief that you would like to have about your creativity or identified issue. Notice where in your body you feel it most.

2. Beginning at the base of the spine, bring your hands to each energy center while stating the new belief as an affirmation for the center and its energy. For example, for the root chakra, you might say, "I am safe and secure in my whole being while speaking in front of others." For the third chakra, one affirmation is "I feel my power and effective assertiveness while speaking to audiences."

Installing desirable beliefs through the chakras.

3. Sense your whole being filling with the light of the new belief in each center; breathe fully and stretch your arms wide to the outer dimensions of your biofield. Punctuate with an exultation when you finish.

4. Notice related beliefs that you might want to add; install them in a similar fashion. Make a visual reminder or poster of the most empowering beliefs. Enjoy your new images, talents, and abilities!

Exercise 5.3 Releasing Limiting Beliefs through the Acupoints

1. As you sit or stand comfortably, think of a limiting belief regarding your creativity or another identified issue. Rate the truth of it for you on a scale of 1 to 10 (from 1, meaning it is not very true at all, to 10, meaning it is very true at this time).

2. While stating the belief, tap gently on each of the fourteen acupoints (see figure 3.5) ten to fifteen times while stating, "I now release my limiting pattern of _____."

3. Rerate the truth of the belief for you on the 1–10 scale. Truth for the limiting belief should be very low on the number scale.

4. If the issue has not fully released, you may want to restate the limiting belief making it even more specific, or you may find a related, more emotionally charged belief with which to work.

Exercise 5.4 Installing Desirable Beliefs through the Acupoints

1. Now think of a desired belief regarding your creativity or selected issue. Rate how strong the truth of it is for you on a scale of 1 to 10. If the new belief is less than a strong 10, continue with this exercise. If it's already a 10, give an exultation and install a related belief of which you are not yet as sure.

2. Now tap the fourteen acupoints while stating your new belief out loud.

3. Reevaluate the validity of the new belief with your self-rating. It should be a 10 or close to that; if not, repeat the process, making the new belief even more specific and enjoyable.

Exercise 5.5 The Temporal Tap
for Changing a Psychological Habit

This exercise was originally used for pain control in Chinese medicine. It is also very effective in breaking emotional habit patterns and establishing new resources. It accesses the right and left hemispheres by alternating a statement of a previous, dysfunctional belief while tapping on the left side of the head, with a positively stated desirable belief while tapping on the right side. The exercise involves elements that are powerful for accessing change: repetition, auditory and kinesthetic sensory processing, autosuggestion, neurological reprogramming, and stimulation of numerous meridians on the head.1 As always when working with beliefs, your wording must be consistent with your values and thinking.

1. Starting at the left temple, tap the left side of your head from the front around to below the ear with a few fingers of your left hand. State the limiting belief you wish to change by tapping front to back at least five times while attuning clearly to your words. Example: "I used to believe that creativity was only for the gifted few."

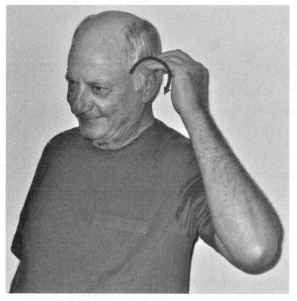

The Temporal Tap starting at the left temple.

2. Now tap with the right hand on the right side of your head from the temple to around the back of the ear while stating a positive version of the belief. Repeat this about five times, while attuning to the meaning of your words. Example: "I now accept my right to be fully creative in my life."

3. Go back and forth several times. Repeat this process several times
    during the day. The more you tap on both thoughts, the more
    you will change the habitual thinking pattern.

The Power of Self-Acceptance

The energy strategies listed so far show person-centered approaches to accessing inner wisdom. One approach is simply acknowledging self-acceptance with affirming statements for energetic balancing while tapping or touching the upper mid-chest: "I deeply and profoundly accept myselfwith all my talents, gifts, and abilities to love." Conversely, positive intentions and internal cohesiveness, even in the face of presumed errors, can be affirmed with the statement, "Even if I make a mistake, I deeply and profoundly forgive myself."

Another resource for self-acceptance is by recognizing alternate learning styles. Creative thinking, as encouraged by learning one of the arts, differs significantly from the analytical modes used in most educational systems. Centering practices permit connecting with one's inner wisdom and increase the capacity for all forms of learning. In effect, focusing techniques bring scattered, disorganized thinking into coherence. By way of analogy, centering is the energetic equivalent of switching from an incandescent electrical light source to a laser. Incoherent light with random emissions wastes energy, whereas the laser light is highly focused and directed. If emissions from a simple light bulb were turned into laser beams of coherent light, they could burn holes into thick sheets of metal. So too, the human mind can become powerful, directed, and inventive when its energies are brought to coherence with mindful centering and positive, helpful beliefs.

****

As you access increasingly effective new intentions for yourself and learn to connect with self-acceptance, you become the conscious

cocreator of your life, the creative artist of your life that you were
meant to be. In succeeding chapters, we'll explore this creative thinking and its gifts for full-energy living.

Chapter Six

Transforming the Energetic Imprint of Daily Grit

Where do we go for our guidance? I suggest that we have no place but our own well. We all have this well inside.
—Marion Woodman

Going to the outside for your energy source, you will always be disappointed because it doesn't last. Finding knowledge within is what is going to sustain your vital energy.
—Susan Taylor, therapist

The basic tool for energetic self-care is identifying problems readily. Dealing with adversity requires awareness of the cause of distress. Denial, avoidance, or wishing problems away do not release an issue's psychoenergetic imprint. Just as physical stress builds up and resentments and personal grudges amass in later life unless we've learned mechanisms for release and forgiveness.

When the energetic imprint of a problem can be released, it will no longer dominate our lives.

Effective letting go means we no longer hold an emotional investment in relating to a difficult situation. Not that we've forgotten the issue or event, but it no longer grips us as intensely. After employing a releasing strategy described in this chapter, a friend noted, "It is as if there is some distance between me and the problem, like a veil. It's not right in my face anymore, and now I can think more clearly."

Intrapersonal Traits for Happiness

The science of happiness in the form of positive psychology emphasizes building on our strengths. "Psychology is not just the study of pathology, weakness, and damage; it is also the study of strength and virtue. Treatment is not just fixing what is broken; it is nurturing what is best."[1] Psychology is not just another branch of medicine; it is an exploration of such experiences as insight, love, play, and satisfactions that make life worth living. Just as physical health is more than an absence of disease symptoms, psychological well-being maximizes inherent potential. Positive psychology has identified the following traits as essential to full-dimensional living:

- Hope, a stance of optimism

- Courage, with pervading curiosity

- Autonomy, ability for self-regulation

- Responsibility, capacity for self-determination

- Perseverance, with resilience in the face of doubt or adversity

- Wisdom, interpersonal skills, tolerance for differences

- Reflection, leading to an inner sense of satisfaction

- Altruism, a quality of generosity toward others

- Creativity, originality, nurturing sense of flow

- Spirituality, trusting in the basic goodwill of the universe

The study of these vital personality traits, and how we might aid others in developing them, is just beginning. Energy therapy practitioners find that positive personal traits often emerge spontaneously once the heaviness of a client's distress is lifted. At other times, positive qualities can simply be encouraged with reminders from friends. Emotionally healthy people want to remove impediments in their lives by learning effective coping skills and amplifying their strengths.

A look at coping patterns shows that it is not so much what has happened to us, but rather how we perceive and interpret life events.

Of vital importance is how we see ourselves after experiencing a personal challenge, difficult diagnosis, or significant loss.

An interesting study showed how peace-loving and spiritual thoughts in early life increased quality and length of life despite later physical illness.[2] Regardless of what health problems a person faces, as long as there is a mindset of positive expectancy, people live better and longer. Optimism about one's health is the most accurate predictor of longevity and quality of life.

Ken's Story: "I Don't Want to Talk about It!"

Ken avoided talking about his parents at all possible costs. His wife said there had been intense mistrust, tension, and unforgiving anger between Ken and his parents during the forty-five years of their marriage. Ken would not discuss with her anything related to his parents.

Ken had been smoking since he was thirteen. He had numbed himself to avoid the pain of his parents' endless arguments. When Ken turned seventy-two, he and his wife jointly decided it was time to break his unhealthy habit of smoking. Ken successfully healed himself from the complex addiction after nine months of working with a therapist who used some of the energetic interventions described here.

Ken still continued to change the subject at mention of his parents. Unresolved conflicts with his troubled, now deceased parents continued to be a major factor, especially in the intensified irritability that arose after he stopped numbing his feelings with nicotine.

The therapist asked Ken to notice bodily sensations while remembering a fight between his parents. Ken immediately noticed a tight feeling in his stomach, accompanied by a sense of fear and nausea. His self-rating for the intensity of the feeling was 8. When the therapist encouraged him to stay with his feelings and sense his grief, the tight sensation released spontaneously. He continued to release the tension of the suppressed feelings by yawning, crying, tapping his whole body, moving to stretch tight muscles, and taking in deep breaths. He then rated his emotion about his parents' arguing as 2.

Tracking the somatic response gave Ken and his therapist a path for accessing long-suppressed material. Releasing much of his inner tension by tracking the stirred up bodily sensations, Ken learned to acknowledge his emotions. He also employed several releasing strategies and continued to use them for several months. Eventually, the emotional intensity of the feelings was 0 as he thought of his parents' scratching fights. The memories no longer created an emotional "charge." He was able to wish his parents well and to ask for their healing at whatever level is possible on the other side. To his wife's delight, his irritability in the present also decreased. Bringing what was unspeakable to light had brought healing for Ken. Problems seem to grow and increase in size like mushrooms when they are held in the dark.

Steps for Transforming Disturbing Issues

Once there is awareness of a troubling situation, we have the capacity to make empowering choices. We start by rating our distress and fully expressing it to a friend, to a consultant, or in a personal journal. Another step is to note where we sense the tension in relation to the body, the chakra, or meridian areas, followed by conscious releasing maneuvers over the disturbed area or with a method that stimulates specific acupoints. We then rerate the distress to note any changes.

Over time, no single distress or unpleasant situation remains as overwhelming or unmanageable as it was in the past. We recognize we can make choices to create a sense of well-being and transform adversity into useful learning. Energetic strategies offer active participation, in striking contrast to the more passive, long-term methods of traditional approaches. Some well-worn strategies people try include talking about problems until everyone (plaintiffs and listeners alike) wear out, ignoring issues until they seemingly go away, or attempting to analyze all of life and its many mysteries until immobilization sets in. Prevarication about issues can lead to actual "paralysis of analysis."

Self-Rating of Distress

A useful tool for tracking distress levels is the simple 0–10 rating method, applied while thinking of a troubling issue. Rating a problem before engaging in a self-help activity will let you know the importance of the issue and how it affects you. Rerating your emotional investment after you have used a self-care exercise will let you know your degree of change. Some issues fall away as you increase self-awareness or use a certain technique; others require frequent repetition for resolution. Some very thorny issues may not lend themselves to self-care approaches. These may best be worked through with an appropriately trained energy psychotherapist (see the resources at the back of the book).

Sensing the Impact of Distress in Relation to the Energy Field

The physical body often registers emotions that are outside conscious awareness. Likewise, a physical sensation may be related to one or more chakras of the subtle energy system. In Ken's story, the sensations of nausea in the stomach were likely related to depletion or a blockage of *qi* in the solar plexus chakra. When he used a spinning motion over the third chakra, Ken was able to release some stored tension in this area of the biofield. With this activity, Ken felt lighter and more in control. He was also able to remember many past incidents related to the tightening knot in his gut. Gradually, their grip on him released, one by one.

Exercise 6.1 Scanning the Body Map

This is an exercise to help you find the area of your body and energy system that is most impacted by distressing issues. It uses intuitive imagery to access a map of your body and the biofield around it.

1. While seated, center yourself with a breath or a peaceful image and set your intention to scan inwardly for areas of congestion, blockage, or depletion. If you have a current problem, briefly focus on it as fully as possible to know its energetic impact.

2. Imagine you have a map of your body before you. While thinking of the worst aspect of the troubling issue, scan the body map slowly head to toe and notice areas you "see" or sense as pink and lively and those that seem gray or sluggish.

3. Without any judgment or interpretation, jot down what you notice and feel.

Releasing Distress

Once you know which part of your body's field is most involved with your issue, you may find it easier to access related emotions. Remember, once any emotion is deeply felt and experienced, it will only last a few minutes. Lingering emotions, such as grief turning into long-held depression, signify either denial or unwillingness to face an issue directly. As you come face-to-face with your emotion and its bodily signal, you can reduce or discharge its grip using one or both of the following exercises.

Exercise 6.2 Chakra Release

1. Focus on the body part most affected by your issue and notice its relation to one or two nearby energy centers. Think of the psychological meaning of that chakra as discussed in chapter 3 and note how it might be connected to the issue at hand.

2. Let your hands move over the affected chakra and rotate to make a counterclockwise spin. As you attune to the emotion brought forth by your issue, intensify the spin and release it emphatically from your right side with expulsive sounds.

3. The more specific you can make your focus for the release, the better. Examples: "I now release my anger at Jenny about making me wait so long" and "I let go of worry that I might outlast my financial capacities."

4. Once a specific chakra has cleared, the area might feel lighter or smoother. You may want to repeat the releasing spin for each chakra, starting at the crown and working downward.

5. Note how you feel after a few minutes of this strategy and jot down your thoughts.

Exercise 6.3 Acupoint Release

This is a general sequence that awakens specific fourteen acupoints related to all of the fourteen meridians (see figure 3.5).

1. After rating your distress level regarding a specific problem, keep attuning to the selected issue while following the sequence. If you like, you can say "I now release_____ (name the issue)" as you touch each acupoint.

2. While thinking about the issue you wish to release, tap or hold ten to fifteen times at the eyebrow points, alternating right and left index fingers. Then tap the outer eyes in the same way, then under the eyes, then under the nose, and under the lip. Next, tap at the collarbone, just below the junction with the sternum; then tap under your armpits. Still attuning to your issue, slap your lower rib cage with open hands. Then tap the inner aspect of the thumbnail (you can use the index finger of the other hand to do this, or bend one hand so that you are tapping both medial aspects of the thumbnail area). Next, tap the inner aspect of the index finger, then the inner aspect of the middle finger, then the inner aspect of the little finger. Still thinking of your issue, tap the side of the hand, the "karate chop" point. Finally, tap the "valley" spot between the last two knuckles of one hand, using two fingers of the other hand or turning one hand so both sides of the hands are stimulated at the same time.

3. Take a deep breath, and release it fully. Now think about your issue and note any change in your distress level.

4. If nothing has changed or you're not sure, continue tapping the spot between the last two knuckles while closing your eyes, opening your eyes, looking to the left, looking to the right (without moving your head), rolling your eyes full circle in one direction and then the other, humming a tune, counting to five, humming again. All these movements help to generalize the release of the problem throughout various brain regions.

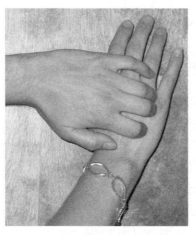

Tapping between the last two knuckles during the Acupoint Release.

5. Repeat steps 2 and 3 and note any changes in your distress level.

Maggie's Story: Spontaneous Memory of Abuse

During her annual physical, Maggie, seventy-five, had spontaneously recalled childhood sexual abuse. Her physician referred her for counseling. Apparently, all parts of her conscious and subconscious mind finally felt safe enough to disclose the terrifying childhood events. Maggie had never been to counseling and was initially very suspicious. With the counselor, she rated the intensity of a specific memory related to her older brother's abuse as 10; in other words, it still felt life-threatening to her even though nearly seventy years had passed and the brother was long deceased. Apparently, it was her time to heal the old wounds and her counselor offered the intervention given in exercise 6.3.

After the first round, Maggie's fear and shame dropped to 5. After a second round, Maggie cried and mentally scolded her brother. By the third round, she felt calmer and agreed to return. During the next session, she reported feeling "at peace" with her brother. She exclaimed in retrospect, "What a dummy he was for messing up most of my relationship life!" The counselor gave her a set of affirmations and specific suggestions for treating her current husband more kindly. Maggie did not return for more counseling, but her referring doctor reported a major breakthrough in Maggie's severe physical pain from diabetic neuropathy.

How to Spark Curiosity and Embed Personal Power

If you are willing to try new ways of responding to everyday challenges, these methods will give you a good start toward self-empowerment. The more specific your focus, the more readily you can let go of a problem's attached emotional intensity. This will allow you to think more clearly and to discover new choices for dealing with similar situations. Your view of a problem can foster a sense of powerlessness or spark curiosity about the many available resources for resolution.

Here's an example: You have a flat tire while hurrying to get somewhere. Your first response may be a strong sense of frustration. Then you have choices to make: to give into the frustration and feel victimized or to say, "Hmm, interesting, what can I do to solve this problem?" You could choose to smooth your ruffled feathers with a Brush Down (exercise 1.2) or energize yourself with the Zip Up (exercise 4.3). You could take a deep breath and affirm that you are capable. You could let go of frustration through a quick chakra spin or by tapping acupoints. It is likely that things will be a little easier as you try out these possibilities.

Certainly, energetic exercises will not add harm or have undesirable side effects. Similar to the work described in the previous
chapter about beliefs, releasing the effects of a distressing problem
is only part of the solution. Further inner work includes willingness
to see ourselves in new ways, to set effective boundaries, to attract
such desirable traits as needed, and to affirm our abilities to handle
problems differently.

Exercise 6.4 Attracting Positive Traits

As you review the bulleted list given at the beginning of the
chapter, decide which quality from positive psychology you would
most like to attract and internalize. You can also think of the problem
situation you have released in light of the strengths and insights you
now wish to manifest. Remember, you have already had some experience with each of these traits at some time in your life because they
are part of everyone's vast human resources. Bringing the selected
trait to the current situation might, however, feel like a new adventure to you.

1. After selecting the quality you wish to activate, start affirming its
    presence in your life through a remembered successful experi-
    ence.

2. Bring the trait to life in your body by tapping each of the four-
    teen acupoints, just as you did in the release work, only this time
    use the phrase, "I now bring in/attract _____ (e.g., courage) in
    facing the situation with ___(give name or specific)."

3. Alternately, you can affirm the presence of the positive trait by
    holding your hands over each of the seven chakras, one at a time,
    starting at the base and thinking of the personal power of each
    energy center.

4. Notice how you feel when you call positive traits to mind and
    make them yours.

* * * *

The mind is very quick at coming up with new images and solutions. One of the hallmarks of personal creativity is to take time to focus inward, access inner wisdom, and respect what comes. The deeper we allow ourselves to reach, the more we become fascinated with the rich storehouse of resources residing within.

Since the world is filled with all kinds of difficulties, there will be endless opportunities to practice newfound skills. As you see opportunity and adventure in new ways of handling day-to-day stress, you will access your innate creativity and capacity for more enjoyment. Sometimes, making lemonade is the very best thing you can do with a lemon!

Chapter Seven
Celebrate the Present!

Only this actual moment is life.
—Thich Nhat Hanh

Whereas guilt and remorse rehearse the past, worry and anxiety are future-bound. Both past and future melt away when we can allow ourselves to fully enjoy the present. Resources discussed so far, such as energy balancing and releasing strong emotions related to a problem, permit a sense of inner peace, even at times of external turmoil. Although being totally in the present is often elusive, even brief glimpses of such moments each day allow us to feel the blessings of the moment. Self-acceptance allows us to feel the rich support of sustained energy from within.

This chapter demonstrates tools to celebrate the present in the following ways:

- Developing an inner practice of mindfulness.

- Noticing beauty.

- Acknowledging positive intentions toward self.

- Making a "bucket list."

- Experiencing the grace of a moment.

- Reaching beyond dualities.

Mindfulness in Daily Tasks

Many programs teach meditation as a process requiring developed skills and repetition. Simply bringing consciousness to the next breath allows refocusing of oneself. Others' ideas might be helpful in getting started, but choosing to be conscious and present at any given moment is the key in whatever path you choose. Mindfulness can become your trusted friend.

Exceptional athletes train themselves to excel in all kinds of weather and terrain. Like "inner power" athletes, your energy resource tools need to be readily available for all situations. Repeated practice gives you the ability to draw on your storehouse of developed skills in the most challenging times.

Breath is the connector between the physical body, the active mind, and the soul essence. Breath is the ultimate connection to our vital life force, called *qi* in Chinese medicine and *prana* in East Indian traditions. Other practices, including centering activities, can be enhanced through deliberate use of the focusing breath.

Exercise 7.1 The Focusing Breath

1. Allow yourself to fully release your next out-breath by releasing it slowly as if gently blowing out a candle. See if you can really empty your lungs to a slow count of 10.

2. Notice how the next in-breath is fuller and deeper. Again, give full attention to just letting go while slowly counting to 10; breathe in while fully releasing in this way three more times.

3. As you continue to breathe more naturally, let go of tension around your eyes, mouth, neck, and shoulders. Imagine any remaining tension and pressures flowing out from your hands and feet.

4. Be aware of the inflow and outflow of the breath while enjoying the present moment. *Now* is all there is. As intrusive thoughts appear, return to the breath and your perception of the unencumbered present.

5. Do this practice daily for five to ten minutes. Allow yourself to feel revitalized and free of intrusive thoughts during this brief moment in time.

As you repeat the focusing breath exercise, it can become easier and more fun. It is similar to giving yourself a vacation from the busy ego without having to travel anywhere. If sitting still is difficult, another option is to walk slowly while feeling the rhythm of the breath. Some people find it helpful to slowly move back and forth in a rocking chair while practicing the focusing breath.

One way to enhance this experience is to bring the focused breath to tasks you regularly perform. Don't rush to get the dishes done while thinking about something else. Instead enjoy focusing on the task at hand: notice the temperature of the water and how it feels to your hands, notice the soap and whether it makes bubbles, notice the gleam on a clean dish, notice the feeling of satisfaction with what you are doing. Be grateful for this very instant. Feel the breath supporting your task. Enjoy this easy, playful moment fully!

Beauty in a Flower

Appreciation of the present expands with awareness of beauty. Nature is full of magical moments and her gifts are unending through nurturing generosity: sunrises, sunsets, springtime's many shades of green, fresh air, smells after a storm, the magic of moonlight.

Unfortunately, many urban environments are quite disconnected from perceptions of nature's bounty and one has to consciously stretch the imagination to find such experiences. Writer Michael Ventura notes, "The experience of beauty is always one of expansion, of opening, of inclusion...So beauty is not merely decorative; its primary function is to connect—beauty connects our innermost being to the world."[1]

Because of our culture's many distortions, we need help in learning to see, hear, and feel more fully again. The following exercises expand appreciation of the surrounding world. To celebrate specific moments just for yourself, you can use one at a time or several in sequence.

Exercise 7.2 Accessing a Beautiful Memory

1. Take a moment to describe the first time you noticed something beautiful in your life. How old were you were at that time and what were you wearing?

2. Notice that time's events: the colors, sounds, and feelings. In your mind's eye, see the whole scene. Notice what felt especially good and comforting to you. Recall what you heard, what was said, or what you said to yourself.

3. Let those feelings become even stronger. Note where you sense them in your body. Jot down the memory with a sense of gratitude for recalling it.

Special occasions are a treasure trove of memory keepsakes. A first snowfall, first look at a waterfall, a trip to the ocean. Even though times have changed, appreciation for everything that contributed to those beautiful experiences can nourish and sustain you now.

Exercise 7.3 Finding Places of Beauty in Your Home

1. Either walk through your home or imagine you are surveying each room. Notice where sunlight first touches the furnishings. Notice through which windows the sun shines at noon. Notice from where the last light of day leaves before nightfall.

2. At any time of day, just stop and look around your home. Enjoy how it looks and feels.

3. Think of a place in your home you especially like. What makes it comfortable? Notice what colors or shapes please you. If there is no such place, ask how might you create one.

Exercise 7.4 Recalling the Events of the Day

1. At the end of each day, remember the places where you sat in your community. Note the colors, pictures on the walls, any unusual furnishings.

2. Think of significant people you saw during the day. See them one by one; remember what they were wearing.

3. Remember a moment when you liked being with one of these people. What made you appreciate the person?

4. Recall a time when something did not go well or when you felt uncomfortable or irritated. Explore what happened and how you might address it differently by using one of the releasing techniques.

5. Remember a time during the day when you laughed out loud or when something was funny.

6. Remember the food you ate. Which food or beverage did you enjoy most? Give thanks for everything that was available to you.

Some people are unaware of their surroundings. They do not notice items of furniture or wall decorations. They may even forget meals they ate. Without judgment or criticism, these exercises help widen perceptions and sharpen mental acuity.

As people become more aware of their surroundings, they often respond by sorting and making room for something more pleasing. Regeneration can result from the simple act of relegating litter to its rightful place. Awareness of your surroundings celebrates and nurtures deeper sensitivities of your soul. Remember, actively responding to beauty and novelty also keeps your brain cells alive and functioning.

Acknowledging Positive Intention

Central to all energetic strategies is the sense of positive self-intention. As a special kind of consciousness, intention supports our desire to enjoy each moment and expand our perception of beauty.

It's helpful to have a clear statement of the heartfelt, caring intention you hold for yourself by making a statement: "I want_____ for myself." The more specific you are the better. The subconscious mind responds best to homely, direct statements that can be repeated and internalized readily.

Exercise 7.5 Stating Your
Caring Intention with the Thymus Tap

1. After relaxing yourself with the breath and using one of the centering practices, think of the most central goal you would wish for yourself at this time. Rather than "I want to be happy, wealthy, and wise," make the statement very specific to your most current inner wish. Examples: "I want to be more self-caring by writing things down," "I want to be fully present when I am with my loved ones when they visit," or "I want to be flexible and resourceful when confronted with adversity, such as_____."

2. After stating your positive self-intention clearly, repeat it several times while tapping lightly on the thymus area of the body (in the upper mid-chest area on the sternum). This anchors the intention to the body while giving an encouraging message to the thymus, the master gland of the immune system.

Tapping on the sternum in the Thymus Tap.

3. Repeat your statement of intention often throughout the day until you easily remember it. Notice how having clear intention helps with everyday decisions and simplifies your choices.

4. When you feel you have internalized your intention and it's an intrinsic part of you, you can enlarge your focus to include new aspects of your overall wellness goal. For example, you might choose, "I want to be fully present even when I am with people who don't understand me, such as _____" or "I want to be self-caring and self-protecting even when ____ happens."

Lizzie's Story: Phobia Release

Lizzie had a severe phobia of snakes. Although she loved nature and was an active environmentalist well into her eighties, she had difficulty walking outdoors because of her fear. I helped her to focus on that phobia while tapping a specific series of acupoints. In a succeeding dream, she saw a beautiful but highly poisonous coral snake. She was able to perceive its exquisite markings in her dream, instead of killing it or running away. Lizzie then found a glass jar and was able to show the snake to her environmental students before releasing it into a wilderness area. This dream was as real as any lived experience and gave Lizzie a great sense of safe, personal empowerment. It was as if her psyche showed her direct resolution to her conflicted fears. It all started with her intention to enjoy nature more fully.

Making a "Bucket List"

The 2008 movie *Bucket List* presented the dilemma of two very different men both faced with a diagnosis of about six months to live. The more philosophical character makes a list of things he wants to do before "kicking the bucket." The resulting adventures as they join forces make lively, yet deeply poignant entertainment.

Because audiences could laugh with the movie, a difficult and often denied topic could be addressed. Laughter is the most direct path to healing. It is exactly what is needed to help us through extraordinarily heavy times. You do not need to tell a joke or have a reason to laugh. It's just fun to be happy. Even if you don't feel that way inside, the brain does not know the difference, so laugh anyway.

No one should wait until a terminal diagnosis to start living more fully. Make a list now of the things you want to do, the people you want to see, the actions you can contribute to make the world around you better. Living with regrets when it is too late to make desired changes generates exceedingly painful emotions.

Experiencing the Grace of a Moment

I was a little down during a week of incessant wintry rain. One day after lunch, I was at loose ends because there was not enough time to start a project before my scheduled meetings. Having nothing to do is rare in my usually more structured days.

I decided to exercise and did the Belly-Button Connection (exercise 4.6), moved my arms in figure-eight patterns, and took some deep breaths, but still did not feel any better. Finally, I dropped in despair down to the ground asking for help. "Please give me a bit of hope, on this super-dreary day. Anything at all will do."

Just then, my gentle cat came over to nudge my chin. Although he often does this, it was rare for him to reach out in the middle of the day, especially just after coming indoors and settling into his blanket on the couch. His timing was perfect, purr-fect. He purred and smooched so much that I turned over on my back to whisper gratitude. At that moment, the dark skies suddenly opened. The sun made a brief, blinding two-minute appearance before the curtains closed again for more of the expected rain.

In my heart, I knew I had asked, and miraculously received, two unassuming gestures from nature. They would be easy to dismiss as mere circumstance. On the other hand, it's easy to accept the grace the moment gave, and feel the joy of a tangible response to my distress call. The rest of the day reverberated with this sense of grace, my connection to deeper life and hope. I had made a choice and, with that choice, I could free myself from despair to see a brighter picture. Miracles await us wherever we are willing to see them.

There's well-known story about a man in a flood who ignored all offers of assistance while praying for divine help. Sometime later he finds himself at the Pearly Gates and demands, "Well, what happened? I asked for help but died instead." The answer boomed back, "Yes, son, I sent you a plank to float on, but you refused to get on; I sent you a lifeboat with helpers, but you declined their offers; even at the last resort, a helicopter came by, but you turned away, saying 'No, thank you, I'm waiting for God to come help me.' So you see, son, by the laws of the universe, you drowned."

We need to seize the opportunity in each moment. Miracles come in many sizes and shapes and seldom look as expected. We must learn to see what is right in front of us and know miracles are possible all around.

Moving beyond Dualities

Many seeming opposites constantly confront us. We experience the interplay of these disparate forces as paradoxes. Here is a sampling:

- Internal needs and external pressures
- Holding on and letting go of control
- Hope and discouragement
- Personal strengths and weaknesses
- Masculine and feminine points of view

- Certainty and uncertainty

- Order and disorder

- Life and death

- Faith and distrust

- Conservative and liberal orientations

- Involvement and apathy

- Expected and unexpected events

- Body and mind

The linear mind wants to make sense of these dualities by choosing one over the other or seeing one as more important. This establishes polarity and leads directly to the root of most conflicts. Yet emotional intelligence, resourcefulness, flexibility, and maturity require learning to tolerate the tension of opposites to find conflict resolution. Solutions come from greater awareness and higher levels of understanding. World-renowned cultural anthropologist Angeles Arrien, PhD, states, "This more accepting and expansive way of thinking increases our tolerance for ambiguity, which is a function of wisdom. The ability to move beyond black or white, good or evil, helpful or harmful, signals wisdom's presence."[2]

If you can look at both of the seeming opposites, you may see how they relate. It is seldom a question of "either/or" but rather one of "both/and." One aspect often requires the presence of its opposite, and both may comprise one unifying truth at a higher level. Wisdom looks for elegant solutions, ones that create win-win situations and serve the greatest good for all concerned. Most far-flung families of today desperately need an elder who can embody this kind of wisdom. Communities likewise need skillful problem solvers, mediators, stewards, and models of patience and kindness.

My favorite country store was often in disarray. The owner was interested in every new gadget and product. His wife, who waited on customers, often could not find a requested item and would throw her hands up in frustration. After meditating on her wish for order and the store's chaotic disorder, the wife quietly posted a sign reading, "Please appreciate us and bless this mess." A gradual shift occurred: first, she relaxed. Because the nagging ceased, the owner had more energy to organize an index of his supplies. Everyone smiled when they saw the sign. They could relate to its message and grumbled less about waiting. Once tensions lessened, solutions could come. The duality of order and disorder could be tolerated under the umbrella of a bigger, more unifying theme of healthy messiness.

The tension of different ideas and concepts is felt in our physical and energetic bodies. Energy-related exercises can help increase tolerance for confusion, allowing available vigor for new synthesis to occur. The great physician and teacher Milton Erickson often invited his students to "step gently into the middle of nowhere" and be comfortable with "the certainty of uncertainty."[3]

The following exercise invites you to face seemingly opposing forces. The exercise can also help increase your tolerance for dealing with conflicting ideologies.

Exercise 7.6 Reconciling Dualities

1. After focusing with the breath, think of two dualities disturbing you. (If two do not come to mind, select an example from the earlier list).

2. As you view each side of the duality, notice where you most feel bodily tension. Bring your intention for healing to the area you have intuitively selected. Release worry or concern with several downward brushing motions. Allow a sense of warmth and caring to build, like a protective layer, over the part of the body most needing it.

3. Imagine you are at a vantage point above the two opposites. Imagine the two opposites talking to each other while you are a referee for conciliation.

4. As you feel your own center and energy flow, imagine what a revered teacher, such as Jesus, Mary, Buddha, Lincoln, or Gandhi, would say.

5. Enjoy the sense of your centered state while viewing the seeming opposites. Jot down insights as they come to you.

Much as we cherish security and certainty, realistic people recognize there are no guarantees. Given today's global tensions, ever-recurring anxieties about the future seem to be a given. You can treat anxieties energetically by rubbing the tender spot on the upper left chest and repeating, "Even though I feel anxious about the future (or name a specific issue), I deeply and profoundly accept myself." You can release anxiety from each chakra area (figure 3.3) or by tapping all of the fourteen acupoints (figure 3.5). You can learn to tolerate the tension of opposites by installing empowering beliefs. The power for change lies within you and your creative energies, not in some external, wished-for change.

As you develop genuine inner confidence in facing dualities, the stamina and generativity needed for social activism can be accessed. Much cooperative work, both internally and with others, is required to become true stewards of our fragile planet. Quality of life and future sustainability cannot happen without our full participation. Thankfully, wise elders who can tolerate differing points of view are beginning to significantly influence needed societal change.

****

Fear-based thinking might encourage someone to seek security by buying more insurance or building higher emotional walls. In truth, there is no guarantee of absolute safety. Anything can happen to anyone at any time.

The best antidote is to acknowledge the seeming dualities all around us and choose to live fully with hope and caring. We need to trust a deeper wisdom that can cheerfully say, "Bless this mess" and "Expect the unexpected," and know we will still be all right at some level. As you use the suggestions given here, you access flexibility and inventiveness, as well as your human birthright to be present in the moment.

The next chapters invite you to find your inner sparks of creativity. As you read on, allow yourself to fully enjoy every moment in the adventure of becoming the artist of your life!

Part III:
How Personal Creativity Relates to Well-Being

Chapter Eight

Gardening in the Desert— Developing Personal Creativity

Being creative is about coming to the canvas of our lives with delight, abandon, and unthwarted, untrapped imagination. It's about using our gifts in the service of others, extravagantly, from our center.
—Jan Phillips, human relations teacher

Meaningful work, service to others, creativity and personal health are closely linked. Unless you tend to the creative fire within, you will not have the energy, vitality, and resourceful inventiveness needed to actualize your life dream. Depression, stagnation, and despair all too often dominate later decades of life. Major questions to consider for optimal aging are: What do I want to contribute to this world? What is my legacy to future generations? What do I really love to do?

Sarah's Story: From Family Cast-off to Animal Lover

Sarah had become thoroughly discouraged with her three-generational family. None of them seemed interested in knowing about her needs related to her painful arthritic hands, or in spending time with her; they seemed fully absorbed with themselves and in being successful in the world. One day when she sat crying to herself, an inner voice told her someone, maybe even an animal, might like her companionship. She went to the animal rescue shelter in her town and found not one but several hundred lonely souls, abandoned pets who relished a single kind word or gesture. Sarah was deeply touched by their plight and started reaching out to them. The animals came to her and connected with her deep sense of abandonment. Sarah's darkest moment was the opening to an opportunity. After several days of petting and talking to the cats and dogs at the shelter, Sarah offered to help the other volunteers. She made friends. Family members noted Sarah was often not at home when they called on perfunctory telephone check-ins. By giving her caring to others, Sarah regained her life. Over time, family members were actually interested in her activities and she began to have plenty of stories to tell them. In her despair, she had learned her soul's code.[1]

You need to ask not so much what the world needs, but rather what stimulates and excites your inner fires, what speaks to your soul's code. Because the world needs exactly the unique quality of passion that only you can give.

See What You Can Do!

Here we'll focus on energetic strategies to help you to become the creative artist of your life, whatever your current age. Let's begin by defining "creativity." We are not speaking of unusual talents mysteriously bestowed on only a select few, but rather about our natural potential for seeing things in new ways. Personal creativity as a lifestyle is available to anyone willing to be open to new possibilities. As you work on your life, you will become its artist.

Dr. Angeles Arrien writes, "To generate is to initiate, to inspire, and to originate something that is meaningful, hopeful, and sustainable for ourselves and others. In generativity, we become mentors and stewards. We give back to our families and communities, sharing our wisdom, experience and passion..."[2]

Becoming creative then, is not about producing something or attempting to please others. It's about committing to a daily process of learning, forgiving, reviewing events, and integrating ideas. It's about allowing your life to become your art. As you open up to the transformative potential of each moment, you will learn how to move through inertia or stuck places in your thinking and how to trust your quick mind and its symbols.

As I reflect, I notice how the creativity of ordinary people doing extraordinary things most impresses me. The prowess of well-known painters can amaze me, but when Darla, who farmed most of her eighty-two years of life, picked up a brush and made a small painting for her grandchildren, I was awestruck.

It is the same with the celebrities of successful aging. One can't help but be impressed with the septuagenarians and octogenarians who dive into icy waters on New Year's Day in Boston and the incredible productivity of elder authors who keep expanding their visions and versatility. When a senior makes a shift from living in drabness to finding something meaningful to live for, as Sarah did, I am most deeply touched.

Personal creativity is available to all of us engaged in the adventure of bringing meaning to the second half of life and bringing our dream to reality. Developing creativity requires mastery of at least one domain and the nurturing of such specific personal traits as openness and resilience. Your chosen domains may be cooking, gardening, knitting, singing, playing an instrument, loving animals, writing, counseling, crafting, interior design, or creating beauty somewhere. Although exploring any chosen domain in depth might bring eventual recognition from others with similar interests, for most of us, mastery of an area of study is simply a way of finding personal fulfillment. Exploring and mastering an interest is enriching in itself, whether or not it evokes recognition from others.

In addition to being a successful computer programmer, Bob nurtured his lifelong interest in the Civil War. Over the years, this led him to many libraries and historical sites, and to meeting others with related interests. Bob's willingness to follow his passion brought him many adventures in addition to personal satisfactions that were missing in his professional career. At seventy-five, Bob is quite an expert on the Civil War, yet realizes there is still much more for him to learn.

There is no limit when we investigate our passions in depth.

Impediments to Personal Creativity

Unfortunately, many of us become disconnected from opportunities for personal fulfillment. Optimal living requires both reclaiming our potential for personal creativity and reconnecting with the innate human capacity for inventiveness. Life offers more than just working through its challenges. Life certainly offers more than just having fun or filling up time with meaningless activity. High levels of well-being can be achieved by channeling self-expression into a creative lifestyle.

A good place to begin accessing principles of creativity is to watch how young children relate to the world. Everything new is fascinating and sparks their curiosity. They explore, play, question, move, shove, tear up, and put things together in new ways. They derive pleasure and satisfaction from building something, then gleefully whamming it down, and then building something grander. They are in a flow—just doing something for its intrinsic pleasure and satisfaction. They give no thought to the future or about what others might think. They are totally in the moment.

Few adults maintain this sense of flow. Fewer still simply enjoy an activity for its own worth, or the possibility for discovery and invention.[3] How can we recover the spontaneity we once knew as children? How can we make time for private projects without any thought about where they might lead us? How can we relearn turning to our inner knowing? How did our playful, explorative, imaginative selves become so burdened in adult life? How can we actively seek ways to counteract trends toward constriction, hardening, and limited perceptions?

From a psychological point of view, early life trauma may be a major factor. Self-esteem and confidence can become eroded in many ways. When there is loss or violation, or when there is lack of recognition and validation, or when persons do their best and no one notices, people tend to feel ignored or invisible. They may come to think of themselves as dumb, incapable, or unworthy.

In addition to negative programming in childhood, our social environment reinforces limiting beliefs about creativity. Beliefs such as these abound: "Oh, I can't carry a tune," "I can't draw," "I'm too awkward to dance," I'm not creative like so and so," "Women aren't good at numbers, and "I could never do that." These beliefs become so internalized we are hardly conscious of their presence. Yet they are powerful influences and require intensive, committed work to reprogram. Fortunately, with our energy resources, there are many ways to release past distress, access more empowering patterns, and nurture innate abilities for creative zest.

Example of Creativity for Survival

In the movie *Cast Away,* actor Tom Hanks captures the psychological truth of the human response to loneliness. Like generations living millennia ago, Hanks, marooned on a deserted island, finds food, establishes shelter, and learns how to make a fire. Although quite alone, he cheers out loud when he succeeds in fire making. He then draws pictures, even a calendar on the walls of his dark cave. They become symbols of his connection with other humans; they are points of comfort in the desperate silence.

A soccer ball, retrieved from a washed-up package, becomes our hero's friend. The lonely man draws a face on the ball, dubbing it "Wilson." It allows imaginary social interaction to take place. Wilson serves as the hero's way of reflecting inner thoughts, thereby helping him access his intuition.

We assume our hero will ultimately be rescued; however, his will to make it happen is a truly creative act. When the castaway unwraps washed-up packages filled with seemingly irrelevant items, we find out ice skates become useful knives, and videotape effectively substitutes for rope. Two sides of a plastic outhouse turn into a shelter and, finally, an effective sail with which he can leave his entrapment.

Observers might say he was lucky to escape the wave-locked island after four years, but one cannot deny the impact of his resourcefulness. The hero made new associations between objects, allowing seemingly useless items to become his tools. He created symbols that empowered him during difficult times and dark nights. He even generated an imaginary friend. He made a map of his location and a calendar based on the times of the year for optimal travel. When the right debris showed up, he was ready to respond and make the most of his preparations.

Traits of Creative People

Discoveries in human history often appear to have an element of luck. But careful observers will acknowledge the years of preparation and willingness to explore that allow someone to move forward when opportunities present themselves. Creative synthesis may follow years of determined effort. Thomas Edison developed more than two hundred models of the incandescent light bulb before he found one that would work. Imagine the persistence and vision required for him to continue through so many seeming failures!

Research proves that highly successful people who become leaders in their professions indeed have extraordinary persistence.[4] Although they may also have certain talents, it's valuable to learn how they persevered, deepened their knowledge, and ultimately responded to fortunate opportunities.

Another trait of highly creative people cited in research is willingness to think outside of accepted, established parameters. Though they are often viewed as oddballs or outsiders, creative people are those who think deeper and venture further than most people.

Seemingly on a lifelong quest of learning and growing, they direct and focus their energies in an enthusiastic search for knowledge and excitement.

Novelty and learning stimulate brain cell development. The fresh connections made with new thoughts not only increase synaptic signals, but actually allow neurons to grow—at any age.[5] Recent research dramatically counters erroneous myths that brain cells do not regenerate or grow. Indeed, the human mind is programmed to expand throughout our lives. As the physical body begins to show limitations, our minds are meant to stretch to novel experiences and ever-greater potentials.

The qualities of novelty and adventure can be cultivated in each of us. As we learn to note strengths and deficits and identify limiting beliefs, we open up more desirable possibilities. The traits of resilience, continuing in the face of adversity, of enjoying each day fully, living courageously even while the body may be weakening, and following new ideas with curiosity as positive options—all these are available to anyone with willingness. Accessing creative self-expression is important for all healing processes. It brings us to new understanding of ourselves and who we are in the world. It takes us beyond just recovering from the past, or our everyday struggles, to the adventure of being fully alive in the present and the future.

As we pay attention to the nudges of curiosity from within and follow our dreams, we certainly will come to feel more content with our lives. It's a safe guess to say we also recharge our inner batteries and our energy systems when we do activities we enjoy.

To explore more fully, let's use a self-inventory to consider the qualities that support originality and creative longevity.

Exercise 8.1 Creativeness Self-Inventory

1. As you review the following list, appreciate the areas to which you are already paying attention and note the ones you would like to develop more fully.

2. Rate yourself on the following items from 1 to 10, with 1 meaning that you seldom do it, and 10 signifying consistent engagement:

- Be curious about something every day.

- Embrace surprises.

- Explore the mysterious.

- Maintain a sense of openness and wonder.

- Consider many subjects that attract you. List at least five.

- Find at least one area to explore in depth and obtain as much available information as possible.

- Be persistent in learning the subject and enhance your skills by moving to increasing levels of complexity.

- Be willing to learn from everything, even what may appear to be a mistake or wrong turn.

- Actively engage in divergent thinking—produce as many ideas as possible, make them as different as possible, consider things from a perspective opposite to your usual way of thinking. (For example, think how another person might see you or your situation.)

- Be flexible.

- Pay attention to feedback so that you can correct your course as you go.

- Organize the mundane aspects of daily life (like knowing where your car keys and glasses are) so your train of thought is not continuously interrupted.

- Take charge of your schedule.

- Cultivate a sense of flow. Take time to reflect. When something sparks your interest, follow it.

- Develop aspects of your personality that are lacking. If you are predominantly rational and analytical, put conscious intention into developing your intuitive senses. If intuition is your strength, consider learning something totally left-brained such as developing more computer skills.

- Know what you like and don't like. List ten things you really like; list ten things you dislike. Enjoy who you are as you connect with permission to express your likes and dislikes.

3. As you review the list again, prioritize one or two items to which you want to give the most attention in the next week. When you incorporate the trait or activity into your lifestyle, select another as your target for the following week, and so forth.

To continue with this as a self-exploration exercise, you might also select the trait(s) that seem most difficult to achieve. For example, taking charge of your schedule to have time for reflection might trigger several limiting beliefs: "Others' needs are more important than mine," "Others' schedules matter more," "There is never enough time for my needs," "I don't deserve to just sit still," and "I'm incapable of controlling my time." Attract desirable, more empowering beliefs by allowing yourself to generate four totally opposite thoughts. Examples might be: "It's not my job to please others first," "Others' schedules affect me only as I choose," "I now make time for my needs," "I decide and take charge of my schedule," and "I am capable and effective in controlling my time."

Each of these new, desired beliefs generates a host of related possibilities. Each may require decisions and further work in setting clear intention and goals. Defining yourself as the artist of your life is, however, an exciting, ongoing endeavor. It will help your brain cells grow! It will be worthwhile for sure because you are worthwhile!

Carol's Story:
Exploring a New Interest toward the End of Life

Carol was diagnosed with a form of leukemia that, while progressing slowly, brought the end of life into clear perspective. She had been a piano teacher before retirement and wanted to learn more about organ music "someday." The diagnosis brought a strong wake-up call: "Someday" would have to be now or never.

She asked herself: "Where could I start to learn about organ music?" and "Which composer could be my guide into learning more about this instrument?" Having always had a strong affection for the work of Bach, whose piano compositions she had studied in her youth, she dug thorough her files for some of her old music and notes. To her surprise, she found a book of more than 370 chorales in perfect four-part harmony written by Bach for piano or organ.

Carol started playing the chorales. She found how the sublime arrangements lifted her soul. She then asked for permission to practice at her neighborhood church. The congregation's young organist offered to give her lessons. As time progressed, the church choir asked her to accompany them on special occasions. Carol's life became filled with glorious sounds both in church and at home. When she passed on several years later, her closing inner peace was enriched with Bach's magnificent music.

Exercise 8.2 Solidifying Your Intention

After you have done the self-inventory, this exercise anchors your newfound intention in your body and mind.

1. Choose one item from the inventory in exercise 8.1 for your focus here. Decide how strong your current skill is in relation to the chosen option. Rate its current strength (10, or 100 percent, being the strongest you can possibly imagine). Example: "I want to find my keys or glasses every time instead of hunting for them all over the house. Current level of success: 40 percent."

2. Tap gently on the mid-sternum area fifteen to twenty times while stating your intention to increase skills related to the selected item.

3. Repeat this affirmation with the tapping as often as you wish, especially when you have successfully accomplished the new skill, such as finding your keys or glasses readily. Note how your skill level improves with the novelty of this exercise and its practical applications.

4. Intensify your connection to the item or select a new one from your list to work on next.

****

Creativity, which honors your vital life force, is at the heart of a satisfying, optimal second half of life. We have considered how novelty nourishes not only the soul, but also brain physiology. Structures for a continuously expanding mind at any age are in our genes and our destiny. We can choose to activate these potentials throughout our lives.

Traits leading to more original, innovative thinking can be further enhanced by increasing intuitive perceptions, connecting more fully with nature, celebrating each moment with hope, nurturing the inner life and artist, and opening to our transpersonal, spiritual dimensions. In the following chapters, we will consider these possibilities with the help of related exercises.

Chapter Nine
Inner Artists at Risk

Make your own recovery the first priority in your life.
—Robin Norwood, author
All the arts we practice are apprenticeship. The big art is our life.
—M. C. Richards, commentator

As you explore ways of becoming more fully yourself, you may recognize that everyone is in some form of recovery. Like others, you may need to integrate and reframe past stressful events. You certainly need to acknowledge your strengths and expanding capacities. You may also need to make peace with internal detractors who deny or interfere with your creative potential. The vulnerable part of you that was criticized or ignored in the past is now called on to recover and step forward. The dignity, grace, and authentic power of true elderhood calls you to become the artist of your life!

This is not easy when we live in an external environment filled with criticism, negativity, and challenges. Additionally, we need to address *intrapersonal* conflicts, those happening within ourselves, such as confounding self-talk, habitual beliefs, and the inevitable inner critic. Care and nurture of the inner artist requires gentle and persistent attention; in fact, it is central to developing the art of living fully at any age.

Tracy's Story: Dancing Beyond Self-doubt

Tracy loved to dance and excelled in her classes in grade school. When she went to high school, however, the natural self-consciousness of a teenager and criticism from peers brought her to self-doubt. Her dancing stopped for many decades. Her second chance appeared in a retirement center with regularly scheduled line dancing events. All her friends made the Saturday dances a highpoint of the week. Nagging self-doubts had to be put to rest—and quickly. Tracy learned ways of releasing old beliefs about herself and her dancing by using the energy psychology methods suggested in chapter 5. It took constant work and firm resolve to show up at the first dance. Her body responded to the music and the joy of the group. She kept surfacing between the dances to exult with her friends. "I can't believe this is me!"

In this chapter, we'll focus on specific ways to:

- Nurture and protect the inner artist
- Set effective energetic boundaries
- Keep the inner critic in check
- Transform seeming failures to learning
- Step into our vision of the future
- Develop flexibility in relationships

Protecting Delicate Plants in Asphalt

We basically live in a culture hostile to personal inventiveness. Consider, for example, the seemingly endless strings of malls in North America featuring the same franchise stores. One could be in any urban area from Seattle to Miami, Toronto to San Diego, and purchase essentially the same products in stores that look alike. There seems to be little value attached to what is unique, special, or out-of-the-way. Although the performing arts are generally recognized as adding quality to life and giving opportunity for cross-cultural communication, funding for the arts is always the first to be cut from budgets. Music and art classes are often dropped from educational planning even though the value of affective learning to train the right hemisphere of the brain is well recognized. The arts are known to be a major contributor to elders' quality of life, but communities must work hard and persistently to keep arts programs viable.

Making something satisfying or developing a new idea from within to expand a sense of purpose requires focused, undistracted attention. Most people still need to recover from childhood trauma related to creativity. The trauma may have been as minor as the wrong glance or word at a vulnerable time, or as major as emotional or physical abuse in front of an entire group. Much like the well-known therapeutic work to recover one's inner child, developing a relationship with the inner artist requires ongoing dialogue and caring.

For most in recovery from early-life criticism, the inner artist is young, easily offended, and prone to quick withdrawal. The seedlings of self-expressive attempts must be nourished with the same mindful gentleness, tolerance, and kindness one would give to raising specialty flowers in unsupportive environments.

Attention to intuition is one way of valuing and nurturing new ideas. We can give permission to honor the wisdom from within as it unfolds. Bringing the imaginative into form is seldom easy, but we can rest assured that each endeavor gets better with repeated practice. When there is willingness to learn, we can and do improve over time.

It's all right for us to be doing something just to enjoy the sense of flow and inner harmony it brings. It's all right to make a mistake, get messy, take risks, and start over when we are engaged in flow, an ongoing process of generating new possibilities and finding personal satisfaction.

As participants in the fast-paced life of the twenty-first century, we are continually bombarded with media advertising that emphasizes thinking and acting like everyone else, and, preferably, younger. This is not just a quiet invitation to sameness; it is a persistent, ever-repeated, pressing demand. It's so pervasive that those who want to envision other possibilities, such as the dignity of eldership, have few guideposts and become numb or withdraw. Thinking "outside the box" and coming up with new ideas is an act of courage in the face of thinking dominated by fear of aging and by youth-related self-interest.

Anyone who ventures forth to generate a meaningful lifestyle different from the norm may be subject to disapproval. It is very easy for a parent to invalidate a child's innovative gestures and to silence curiosity; it is also easy for adults, especially seniors, to intimidate each other. Since so many live in structured neighborhoods, there is ample opportunity for competitiveness, outdoing one another, or finding one's identity by putting others down.

As artists of our lives, we are called to generate substantial backbone, a "thick hide," and courage. The inner artist is at high risk, and we must actively become its protector and sustainer.

The Protective Bubble for an Effective Boundary

Although it is currently invisible except to clairvoyants and high technology, the biofield is a powerful resource for sensing inner strength and coherence. In addition, awareness of this field can help set clear personal boundaries to prevent absorbing "groupthink" or projections from others. Focus on the biofield can help to create an invisible shield, akin to a protective bubble. Further, it can assist in differentiating the useful from what does not fit for you.

You may have noticed how many effective speakers use arm and body movements while they are addressing large groups. Intentionally or not, they are using body gestures to define their energy field and to make sure that they are not undermined by distractions. Protective shielding is important so we don't unconsciously come under the spell of undesirable influence or pressure from others.

Exercise 9.1 Setting the Protective Bubble

This exercise uses imagery of your biofield as a protective barrier to bring in helpful communications and allow other material simply to "bounce off."

1. Think of a recent incident in which you wish you had been stronger in standing up for yourself or you noticed that another person's opinion weakened your resolve. Think of what you might like to have said or done. Remember, "hindsight is better than no sight." Through hindsight we learn to respond more effectively to similar situations in the future.

2. Release several deep breaths fully, letting go of the stress or pain the situation caused in you. Brush the part of your body that seems to be holding the tension. Forgive yourself if needed.

3. Connect with the breath to your central energy line and sense your aliveness from the base of the spine to the top of your crown.

4. Continuing with a steady breathing pattern, sense your energy field, expanding from the center, to the subtle outer layers. Define the size of this biofield with your arms. Move your arms all around to get a three-dimensional sense of this field. Imagine talking and walking with this field as your protective shield.

5. Affirm that this field will automatically select helpful suggestions and ward off irrelevant or harmful material. If you wish, see the field as a dynamic, selective membrane. This membrane has the flexibility to become stronger and thicker, even like steel, when you are around toxic people or situations, and can become thinner, more transparent, when you are with friends.

6. Imagine stepping into this strong protective field for any situations such as the one you identified in step 1. Begin sensing your field whenever you feel exposed or overwhelmed. Feel the breath supporting the protective field.

7. Enjoy a newfound sense of freedom and inner power. Become comfortable letting things that do not pertain to you bounce off.

Anna's Story: Setting Boundaries

Anna used this exercise repeatedly to overcome codependency with her parents and other authority figures in later life. As a child, she had learned to pay careful attention to every nuance of the adults' communications so she could please them and keep peace. She became a "parentified child," the caregiver of her parents, at an early age. In adult life, Anna continued to absorb others' feelings as her responsibility. She was constantly apologizing, making excuses, trying to fix matters, even in areas not her concern. In short, she was continually overwhelmed with others' burdens.

When I asked Anna to imagine a protective bubble to create an effective boundary, she immediately came up with a fascinating image. She saw the protective layers of her biofield as the layers of netting from her childhood ballet costumes—fluffy yet strong, light but sturdy, with webbing that held its permanent shape. This image gave her a defined sense of strength and allowed her to deal with her overly demanding, very elderly parents without succumbing to impossible demands. She was able to say, "Since I can't do all of these tasks at once, which one is most important? What is a realistic time frame? When do you want me to get back to you?"

As her confidence grew, Anna dealt more effectively with her parents and other people's demands. It was a gradual process, taking several months, sustained by the unique boundary-setting image Anna generated in an instant.

Daily Renewal

Inner artistry requires daily refreshing. It's easy to become distracted with life's challenges at the very time when connection to center is most needed. The human soul seems to have a "homing device" because we can always feel relief when we meditate, use centering practices, focus with the breath, or acknowledge ourselves.

One of the skills taught in self-hypnosis is to use regularly occurring body signals to remind us of our need to center so we can release pressures and bring in new possibilities. The breath is natural for this since it happens both with our conscious control as well as automatically. The exchange of air, releasing carbon dioxide and bringing in new oxygen, serves as a metaphor of the need to let go of the stale and make room for the refreshing. Every time we consciously breathe and exhale, we are reminded of our physical health and the integrity of our energy resources. Other bodily functions such as eating, drinking, and releasing waste can also serve as reminders of the constant process of taking in and letting go. As we release what is not needed, we make room for new possibilities and inspirations.

The following exercise uses these reminders to enhance an ongoing sense of personal *qi* and, with it, opportunity for effective self-talk and listening. You might use it as a walking meditation or whenever you feel the need to pull yourself together.

Exercise 9.2 Making Room for the New

1. Use the out-breath to let go of tension. Let tension flow out of muscles that feel tight.

2. Imagine bringing in new possibilities with the next inhalation. Image the inflow of life-giving oxygen to the lungs; see the flow of rejuvenated blood to the heart muscle, the aorta, the head, the torso and vital internal organs, arms and hands, abdomen and pelvis, thighs, legs and feet.

3. Remind yourself, "With every breath, I return to my center. With every breath, I recreate myself. With every breath, I generate new options."

4. Similarly, bring in vital energy as you eat or drink. When you use the bathroom, recognize you're making room for new fluids and foods to energize the body and mind.

5. Remind yourself, "With every drink of water, I refresh my energies. With every food item I eat, I nourish my effectiveness and capacity for a full life. With every new thought, I replenish myself."

Because these concepts are related to bodily functions, they are easy to remember. The next inspiration is literally as close as the next breath (pun intended!). As you practice affirmations associated with bodily activity, you will note your self-talk becomes much more friendly. And it's always good to listen to and write down what comes to you.

Meeting Endeavors with "Eyes of the Heart"

Contrary to popular belief, successful people often fail. But they learn from their mistakes and move forward. They avoid getting stuck. They transform actions that did not work into something useful for future reference. Learning from apparent failures is the most direct way to change perspective.

Much as we did when we were children first learning to ride a bicycle, we may have expectations of successful outcomes without having the necessary skills. This does not mean giving up. Over and over, despite spills my grandchildren get on their bikes, and gradually learn to use their balancing muscles. I have found that the less outside interference in such situations, the better; making mistakes when others are watching generates anxiety or undue sympathy. Encouragement and support, on the other hand, with validation at even the smallest attempt, can be very helpful.

Sometimes all that is needed is to remind struggling persons they are on their way, they are learning, and the process of learning is the lesson. Years of piano practicing let me know that I could get better at anything to which I applied determination. Piano teachers must be among the most patient and nurturing of people. I still remember each of them and their kindness to me while firmly and persistently urging me to practice the same passage one more time. Somewhere along the way, I also learned to have fun and to overcome intense fears of public performance. I still get anxious, however, and treat myself by tapping acupoints and repeating affirmations.

Those who are active in visual or performing arts know the power of repeated learning from mistakes. As the idea or image is reworked, the project becomes more defined, new skills are incorporated, and the outcomes are more pleasing. To presume anything will be ready after one attempt ignores the vast potential for learning at any life stage.

Gretta's Story:
Encouragement to Paint the Healing Picture

Since most adults don't take time to draw, write, or play an instrument in the busy first half of life, attempts at a new endeavor require nourishing environments. Gretta, a seventy-eight-year-old participant in my Monday morning art group, had a long, unusual dream about a large hill with houses and many churches on it, illuminated by a bright pulsating sun. The image was very comforting to Gretta as it came when she was in the midst of turbulent changes related to loss of her husband of fifty-five years. She wanted to hold on to the memory and its good feeling.

"Why not paint it? We'll help you," offered the members of the group. Although Gretta had no previous skills at landscape painting, she put down what she had seen as best as she could. Turning what she really wanted into a satisfying picture took several months and classes, but we all supported her efforts. Trusting the wish for something new became Gretta's present to herself.

None of the suggestions given Gretta would have been acceptable had there been judgment or criticism. People quickly give up on new projects unless there is a strong voice of support. I suggest greeting any new endeavors by yourself or your friends with "eyes of the heart"—a soft, loving quality of nurturing the inner artist while holding open the possibilities of further exploration. Nonjudgmental groups help create learning environments.

Holding Beginner's Mind

Trying out new adventures and exploring art forms while providing careful protection and nurturing may sound like a paradox. Childlike thinking has a playfulness that permits building up and tearing down, trying the new without attachment to outcome. Adult and parental thinking is more structured, moderated by attention to outcome and results, planning ahead to cover contingencies. Recovery of the inner artist requires both ways of thinking, but not necessarily at the same time. The critical, evaluating aspects of the personality must be held at bay temporarily while playing and exploring. More discriminating aspects are needed to complete a project or seek new techniques and methods. The constant interplay between these aspects generates tension that can be helpful in motivating curiosity.

Having the right resources available is one way to foster your creative process. It sets the environment for expressive opportunities. If you wish to get better at writing, have notebooks, writing materials, and computer skills at hand. If you like to work with your hands, get clay, wood or sculpting materials. If you wish to speak in public on a favorite topic, join a group or class with similar interests. Develop opportunities to demonstrate what you are learning. Find supportive friends who accept your endeavors, no matter how awkward. Get feedback from objective persons only after you have overcome shyness about being a beginner.

When you have an idea you want to capture or you have a dream you want to follow, turn the inner artist loose. At first, even five minutes of unqualified playtime might seem like a huge achievement. As you keep repeating the playfulness, the activity may become more complex. You may get a sense of enjoying what comes just for its own sake.

This integrative thinking—childlike play with adult awareness and protection—requires calculated risk-taking. With a relatively small investment of time and money, you can explore dormant interests. Usually, simple projects are at first the most likely to generate satisfaction.

John, a retired massage teacher, was a "hidden poet" who surfaced once a year to send all his friends a greeting at the spring equinox. It took him most of a year to refine the new annual poem idea and to select a pleasing greeting card for this endeavor. John reported feeling ready for the new year after sending out his greeting to his ever-growing mailing list. Feedback from the project was wonderfully encouraging although John never planned to become a full-time writer. "It's just a lot of fun to work on this every year; it gives me a goal for my creativity," he commented.

All too often, however, adult ambitions to succeed, produce something of value, or find recognition take over. Like many parents who wish their children to succeed without teaching them the painstaking steps involved, some may rush out and buy expensive equipment, hoping they will become inventive. A friend of mine thought he would like to do woodworking and, on this whim alone, bought the most expensive set of tools he could find. Unfortunately, he did not take the time to learn how to use the tools, how to select the correct woods, or how to develop woodworking projects. Now everything sits gathering dust in a closet. He laments, "Well, I tried, but nothing much happened."

Accessing the inner artist is a balancing act. Careful intention to be playful and create unstructured time is needed. In addition, it's plain good sense to minimize risks by finding instruction before becoming bogged down or frustrated. Otherwise, it's possible to feel engulfed by expectations and attachments that can lead to giving up prematurely. Holding "beginner's mind" without expectations is a fine way to greet new endeavors.

Challenges Build Muscle

Every life challenge, no matter how devastating it may appear at the time, has within it seeds for new learning. When I work with people who have faced severe abuse or pain in their early lives, recovery involves accessing the positive resources they have already developed as survival strategies. Counselors don't invent new solutions for clients, rather they help remove impediments and find ways to access inner resources.

Once and only once, I met a client who had a charmed life. Everything was perfect for Julie until the sudden death of her husband when she was sixty-seven. She was devastated and bitter because nothing had ever challenged her beliefs or comfort levels. Being blessed with a peaceful life left Julie unable to cope with real tragedy. She had few known inner resources, and gaining insights to work through her grief took much effort.

Unmet needs of the past also need to be addressed. With the help of awareness and increased time in later life, past wounds can indeed be healed. The saying "It's never too late to have a good childhood" is true!

Here is an exercise that allows you to bring your resources for healing to a disconnected, earlier part of yourself and to bring them forward into your future.

Exercise 9.3 Healing Old Wounds

1. After relaxing and centering yourself, think of a time in your life when you felt very challenged. Recall for a moment the feelings of loss, anger, or grief you felt.

2. Imagine seeing the younger person you were at that time in front of you. Notice how the younger person looks and what is needed to bring help.

3. From your heart center, let caring flow to the younger self. Forgive whatever may still be holding this younger person back. Let your caring and comforting surround your younger self.

4. Recall the things you have learned since the time of distress and speak them out loud or write them down. (Example regarding a bad investment: "I learned to take much smaller risks, to find out more about the investment and the investor, and to do much more research before committing funds." Example concerning a lost relationship: "I learned to be more caring, to recognize there are many unknown factors in the development of a dynamic, ongoing relationship, and to humbly admit that I was not in control of the other person.")

5. Consciously give thanks for the learning that has come from the dilemma of the past. Develop an image of seeing yourself moving into the future while bringing forward the things you have learned.

6. Instead of a rusty old barge dragging debris from the past, see yourself as an upscale cruise ship with all the latest amenities, including the wisdom of the valuable lessons you have learned.[1]

7. Enjoy living with this new image of yourself while making sure the lessons you have learned are well embedded in body and mind. One approach is to reiterate what you learned as you focus on each of the seven chakras (see figure 3.3). Another approach is to tap the fourteen acupoints (see figure 3.5) while repeating the learning until it becomes a natural part of your thinking.

8. Write down your lessons as a reminder of the wise person you are becoming; acknowledge the many things you are doing now to integrate the past and help yourself.

Developing Flexibility in Relationships

Undoubtedly, the work you are doing to maintain daily energy balance and to accept your life lessons will impact the quality of your relationships in a positive, generative way. Conscious choosing will increase your sensitivity and flexibility toward others. Any relationship dyad—romantic couples, long-term partners, parent-child interactions, grandparent-grandchildren relationships, connections between colleagues and/or volunteers—can be enhanced by forgiveness and acceptance.

Here is an exercise that builds on the skills you have developed and allows you to extend your consciousness to another person. It brings direction to the art of unconditional love and mutual respect. This exercise can also be done at a distance with someone with whom you feel a close personal connection. You can arrange a time with mutual agreement for the energetic connection and to share your experiences later.

Exercise 9.4 Heart-to-Heart Connection

1. While sitting comfortably across from a person with whom you choose to do this exercise, release the breath fully, and bring your focus into the present moment with a centering practice.

2. "See" the person with the eyes of the heart, noting the soul qualities within rather than external appearance. Notice how this person is similar to you, having, like you, needs, goals, desires, and disappointments. This other person mirrors your own humanity.

3. Let your heart chakra be open with acceptance for the soul qualities within the person. Let your hand stretch out to the other person's heart center to send out your sense of caring.

Heart-to-Heart Connection.

4. As you put forth your mindful intention, let yourself sense the other person's regard for you. Receive the influx of the acceptance with your other hand near your own heart center.

5. Notice the flow of energy between the hands and the eyes. You may feel the connection as an image of a rainbow, a bridge, or a gossamer thread.

6. Sense the wholeness of the other person as you respect and accept your own right to health and healing. Notice how differences of opinion or lifestyles seem less important as you see the other person's deeper qualities and sense your own being.

7. Share with the other person what you learned.

This exercise is a powerful way to overcome long-term obstacles to relational healing. I have used it many times with couples who often have a long laundry list of complaints about each other. Rather than letting them tell me how awful the other person is (they can write lists later if they wish), I teach them to balance themselves by feeling the central alignment (exercise 4.1). I ask them to remind each other to practice energy balancing regularly. Then I ask them to sit with each other as described and to notice each other's deeply human qualities. This allows energy to flow between them, and often they can again find appreciation for what originally brought them together.

One dyad I worked with was a mother-daughter relationship punctuated by sixty-two shared years of nitpicking and anger. The mother, Hannah, and her daughter, Joy, could not sit in the same room without shouting hostilities, although individually they agreed they loved each other. I first taught each of them personal boundary setting with the protective bubble so each could hear what the other had to say without becoming totally disoriented. Then I had them sit with the heart-to-heart connection to sense mutual respect and each other's presence. Joy reported, "I don't think I ever saw my mother as just another human being; I had her on a pedestal and therefore I always wanted to knock her down." Hannah reflected, "This time, I felt my daughter's inner light without all her personality quirks and irritants. I realize her judgments of me are only a small part of who she really is."

As we heal our relationship with ourselves, we also reshape interactions with others. The ongoing presence of intentional *qi* is the force connecting us. As we increase awareness of our *qi*, we generate creativity in the art of relationship and conflict resolution.

****

We've explored specific ways of nurturing and protecting the precious spark of creative thinking that lives within. As you strengthen boundaries and increase relational sensitivity, you open doors to your ongoing evolution.

Chapter Ten
Harvesting Inner Wisdom

When we paint, and when we can let go, the brush begins to dance.
It is our inner beauty that we meet.
—Marie-Louise Ertle, art teacher

O ur intuition, or inner wisdom, is a wonderful addition to personal creativity. The same caring attention we would use in developing relationships with any companion or close friendships over time, is required to build and nurture inner knowing. A whole world of wonder can unfold when we pay attention to thinking beyond usual, analytical thinking styles. Inner wisdom pays attention to little nudges from within, to hunches, educated guesses, or subtle sense perceptions. Having an experience that confirms inner knowing allows us to become more receptive and trusting.

The great psychologist and teacher Carl Gustav Jung described intuition extensively. He recognized its presence in native cultures around the world. Coining the word "synchronicity" to signify the coming together of inner knowing and external events, Jung gave in his writings numerous examples of synchronicities.1 One example was of a woman who had a strange dream she was not sure she could trust. In the dream, a large June bug rapped on the window as if to give her a message. As she retold the dream in therapy, there was an interrupting noise at the window. Both therapist and client looked in amazement as a large June bug flew against the glass. Remarkably, the June bug showed up in March, which is not its usual flying season. With the help of this intersection of events, the woman began to trust in her dreams and move forward with her life.

I've learned to pay attention to both my internal hunches and external signals. When clients share material offering little immediate resolution—addressing deep grief, for instance—I've learned to pay attention to both my inner voice and anything helpful from nature. Once I asked a newly widowed man to read aloud messages on comforting cards sent by loved ones. As he did so, we heard a bird singing outside. It was as if its song supported his process at the moment. Both of us were deeply moved just listening to the song. We felt we had received a message of hope.

Another time, I asked a very scattered lady to do something nonverbal. My words seemed to confuse rather than reach her. I then handed her some crayons and paper. Instantly, she shifted toward a calmer, more centered state. I had no idea that she was an artist who had not drawn for ten years. Through this activity, she began to rediscover her self-esteem. Each week she proudly brought her productions to the painting group. Later, I made a relaxation tape she could play twice a day while painting.

Paying attention to intuition and synchronicities has made my personal and professional life fascinating and full of surprises. As I look for new possibilities, they do indeed present themselves.

You may recall playing a hunch that proved right on. Or you may remember thinking about someone just as the person called you. You may have received mail from a friend about whom you were often thinking. You may also have experienced a series of events that pointed you in a new direction. Although you could not see it clearly at the outset, in retrospect, there appears to have been a plan which went beyond your conscious knowing.

Intuition acknowledges the positive intent of the psyche, which stores far more information than cognitive, analytical thinking. The nonlinear, intuitive mind makes hundreds of connections between life experiences we may not fully comprehend. It brings together ideas through integrative, analog thinking processes. Creative ideas emerge from the mind's rich storehouse, using both left and right brain hemispheres and connecting linear and analog thinking modes.

Redefining yourself as someone who makes an art out of living requires several direct ways of learning about your inner wisdom. One is paying attention to your dreams. The other is keeping a personal journal. Other activities to further strengthen your perceptive skills and expand your resources for open-ended thinking are described in the exercises in this chapter. They include developing your inner dialogue, asking for feedback from others, and making spontaneous object arrangements.

Learning to Trust Positive Intention

Blocks to creativity in the form of limiting thought patterns are usually self-imposed. As the impediments are removed, vibrant energy for new endeavors can emerge. It's renewing, like a breath of fresh air, to see the true jewel residing within.

Most programs related to creativity "for older adults" or "seniors" fail to address the vast repositories of self-doubt many have carried throughout life. Self-criticism resides within many people and hobbles their capacity for enjoyment. Most of us need to rediscover parts of ourselves we never really lost. Several books suggest accessing our internal truth and creativity through poetry writing.[2] By ceasing negative self-talk and making some kind of acceptable peace with the inner critic, we can begin to achieve what we have been putting off.

Adults easily forget the fun of playing with words, paint, clay, dirt, rocks, musical instruments, or clothes. During the medieval hundred years of war, villagers protected their churches' treasures by covering them with ugly lead. Later generations peeled off the lead and rediscovered the gold underneath. Similarly, we can recover the playfulness, the gold inside, we've always had. Remember, when we release energetic blockages, true beauty from within can emerge.

Writing It Down

Journaling about the emotional impact of everyday events is the most readily available tool for self-reflection. All that is required is a notebook and willingness to write down thoughts and feelings. Although a number of books available about journaling may be helpful,[3] a desire to do something regularly for yourself is most central. If you write letters (or e-mails) to friends, why not write letters to the best friend of your life—yourself?

The focus of your notes to yourself need not be descriptive of actual events, although it may be fun to list what you did and how things went. Reflecting on what went well with a sense of gratitude is a good starting place for increasing awareness. Then you might include what did not go so well and begin to generate better options for the future. Themes may begin to emerge: What happens repeatedly? How could it be handled in a different way?

The journal can become a place to record your innermost feelings, a place to reflect on things you might not ever want to share with anyone else, even your intimate friends. Looking at the emotions generated within you gives a direct tool for self-understanding. You may begin to notice how certain events, such as family-of-origin gatherings, always upset you and/or cause psychoenergetic imbalance. Armed with this awareness, you can begin to design family gatherings more to your liking. Lower expectations, less contact time, more structured activity, more proactive centering activity, and more willingness to "be in the flow" are all likely options you can intentionally choose to explore.

Dori's Story: Power in a Change of Heart

A musician friend, Dori, has kept journals since her late teens. Over time, her scribbled notes became a record of her concerts: the good, the bad, and the ugly feelings generated before and after a performance. At a recent dress rehearsal with her group, things went badly. There were numerous mistakes and timing errors. In an effort to recover for the next day's concert, they blamed each other. There were comments such as "Why did this place go wrong?" and "We should have done better" so many times that Dori left the session in tears and with a splitting headache. Clearly, something better was needed.

Writing in her journal, Dori realized how rarely the group members supported or encouraged one another. Something positive would have to happen to ensure a viable performance. With no time for discussion, Dori decided to center herself by bringing in lots of sunshine to her seven major energy centers. She then decided to be very positive with each member of the group before the concert and simply affirm, "I know that everyone is doing their best."

Her attitudinal change paid off. The concert went beautifully. Afterward, the group asked each other how things could have gone so badly the previous day and why the performance went so well. Dori smiled to herself. She knew of the large shift she had made within. That evening, she wrote in her spiral notebook, "Thank you, Dori, for making a good choice and for playing well, too."

Talking Kindly to Yourself

As we continue to increase our self-reflective capacities, we become aware of inner dialogue. The old saw about crazy people talking to themselves has long been superseded. Psychological insights confirm self-talk to be a necessity for emotional health. The nature of the self-talk is important, however. As we witnessed in Dori's example, inner dialogue can be especially helpful in resolving a crisis. Because of past programming, though, many people access an inner critic more readily than an encouraging inner coach. It is not unusual for musicians to attack each other when they feel stressed. In a similar vein, people in all walks of life are quite adept at scolding or berating each other and themselves.

It takes very little to burst the balloon of someone's innovative idea and bring it crashing down to the hard earth. Adults may not give as much power to what others say, but most still have a vocal inner critic, stemming from internalized forms of parental or supervisory admonitions.

We must make peace with the inner critic so intuitive and generative thoughts can emerge. Despite determined attempts, the inner critic does not go away easily. But we can establish a dialogue and make acceptable compromises. The following exercise is one method that has worked well for many of my friends.

Exercise 10.1 Dialogue with the Inner Critic

1. On a sheet of paper, draw a line down the middle and prepare to write on the left side of the paper an activity you wish to do, and on the right side, give room for the critical voice.

2. Select an endeavor you would really like to start but have put off, and write it down. (For example: "I want to write a poem about my dear friend.") On the right side of the sheet, list all the possible objections you can think of. (Examples: "You don't know how to write a poem," "You're not skilled enough," and "No one will like it.")

3. Answer the critic with a dialogue on the left side of your sheet by incorporating new, more empowering beliefs. Then ask the critic what its purpose is and how it wants to help you.

4. Pay careful attention to what you get this time on the right side of your sheet. Jot down the first thought that comes to you; it does not have to make sense. Remember, the intention of your

critic is usually positive: It wants to protect, prevent embarrassment, or help in some other way.

5. On the left side of your sheet, thank the critic for its well-meant intention and state how you really want help now. (For example: "I appreciate your help in wanting me to write well, but I want you to come in after I have written my poem, not before or during my process.")

6. While the critic rests, write down your thoughts about the project as quickly as they come. Let your ideas flow—be they good, bad, or indifferent—until you are finished.

7. When you have completed your project, invite the critic to come in and review, making sure to ask for acknowledgment along with suggestions for improvement. Establish a respectful distance with the critic so that its voice does not overpower your endeavor.

It is easy to see how the critic, if given full reign, could sabotage most original thinking. Fortunately, we have tools for 1) acknowledging the critic and 2) giving it a rightful place as an editor—after a project is completed.

Lenny's Story: Writing to Express Grief

Lenny's poems flowed from expressions of grief over the death of one of his children. They were not meant for others. Lenny emphatically put his inner critic on hold to let himself experience emotional relief by writing about his sadness and anger. Several years later, he reviewed the poems and thought they might help other fathers in similar situations. He called in his inner critic to give helpful suggestions. The poems found a responsive audience among bereaved parents and Lenny's dream of helping others from what he had learned through his loss became a reality. He remembers his unrelenting critic grumbling, "Well, even bad poems can help some people in need." Laughter rippled through Lenny's body when he heard the comment because he noted how the inner critic had softened its previously harsh voice.

Attending to Feedback

Noting the outcomes of any new action and evaluating the result is essential for enjoying creative "fun-gevity." If you made a new investment, you would naturally pay attention to feedback from the market and adjust your course of action. The same principle holds with novel or untried personal ventures, except that the feedback might be a subtler message or a synchronicity from your surroundings.

If we are really not meant to do something, it will prove to be difficult. There may be complexity, timing may feel wrong, or costs may exceed rewards. In such cases, it may be wise to wait awhile and see what else can be learned. In other cases, we get a good feeling and new ideas abound. The timing is favorable, the cost is slight compared to the outcome, and there is often support from others. Such feedback either confirms moving forward or waiting awhile to note what else emerges.

Over a lifetime of working with energy ideas, some projects have taken hold, such as developing the well-known Healing Touch curriculum. Others did not work well at all. In the latter cases, I learned to let go and evaluate how I could avoid repeating errors.

A decade ago, I believed an association for therapists and laypersons interested in energy concepts would be useful. When I met David and Rebecca Gruder, I found friends who had similar ideas. I meditated (consulted with my inner advisor) about a possible affiliation. The meditations were positive. I sent out a trial balloon by asking them their opinion and there was immediate resonance. The three of us decided to start an organization focusing on energy psychology and soon discovered many others who also had a wish for such a group. We found a lawyer to draw up bylaws for a relatively small fee. At the same time that we were finalizing bylaws and reaching out to others on the internet, another therapist had already set up the first international conference for energy psychology to take place in May 1999. Organizing the Association for Comprehensive Energy Psychology toward the end of 1998 was apparently an idea whose time had come. It has been a joyous adventure. We now have more than a thousand members worldwide, sponsor numerous conferences as well as regional events and publications,[5] and have celebrated our tenth anniversary.

The practice of surveying your feedback may involve paying attention to daily nudges to continue doing something or noting when you need to slow down or wait. The following exercise offers some suggestions.

Exercise 10.2 Listening to Feedback

1. Several days after trying out an idea, set your intention for ten to fifteen minutes to gather in the tangible feedback about it.

2. Use the focused breath and a centering practice (see chapter 4) to bring yourself into energetic balance and to feel the connection with your inner wisdom.

3. Jot down or note the things you have done to move your idea forward. (Example: "I mailed a letter to twenty friends announcing a meeting I would like to hold. I set a date for replies and today is the date for that.")

4. Continuing to feel centered and connected with the breath, allow yourself to notice responses to your opening gesture. If the responses were affirmative, you might conclude you're moving in the direction that fits. If there is no response, or it is predominantly negative, you might conclude there is a lack of confirmation at this time.

5. Your response to a seeming lack of confirmation is to make a note of it. Then you might want to explore other options or wait for someone else to step forward with a similar idea.

6. Whether you have received confirmation or not, it's important to affirm your ongoing self-respect: "Even though_____has happened (or not), I deeply and profoundly appreciate and respect myself," repeated at least three times and anchored in the body by rubbing the tender spot on the upper left mid-chest. This ensures staying energetically balanced and attuned to new possibilities as they present themselves.

Noticing Dream Themes

East Indian traditions hold that a dream is akin to receiving a letter from a friend. If we leave the letter unopened, we lose the message from our psyche and its positive intention. If we open the letter and find even a small trace of its message, we can be enriched. Dreams reflect deeper knowing at the subconscious level beyond daytime awareness. Getting to know dream material is another way of enhancing intuition and the connection with the vital life force, or *qi*.

Many people find it difficult to recall dreams, let alone in their entirety. I encourage friends and clients to start by recalling the flavor of a dream—the energy, image, or emotion associated with it—on first awakening. As soon as you change posture or get up, much of the memory dependent on the sleep state is lost. Thus you need to have a pad and pen handy at the bedside, and record what you can remember of your dreams before getting out of bed. Once you develop this practice on a regular basis, you will notice your recall increases.

In working with dream material, it's best to stay away from formulas that define meanings. Instead, find associations with the most meaning for you. Since the psyche is friendly, it often repeats its messages in different forms in recurring dreams. Even nightmares have an underlying friendly message and can bring new ways of looking at problems we are not addressing.

Jerry had recurring dreams about fires. He always woke up before he was burned (because his psyche was friendly to him). Instead of diminishing, however, the dreams increased over a month's time and became more associated with his car. Since he could not make any other associations, he decided to have his car checked. He found out both front brake linings were totally worn and needed immediate replacement. With this experience, Jerry learned to respect his inner wisdom even when it made no sense in the format of recurring nightmares.

The following exercise provides some easy steps you can take to begin making associations with dream material. As the associations become more clear, you will be able to plan activity to integrate the message from the dream into your life.

Exercise 10.3 Making Associations with Dream Material

1. Select a dream with strong emotional impact on you. (Example: A favorite pet is run over and killed instantly.)

2. Connect with the emotion of the dream and turn it into a statement. (Example: "I am distraught that things can happen so quickly.")

3. Think of numerous times in your life when you've had similar feelings and jot down all the associations you can make. (Examples: "I was distraught about the sudden ending of my job," "I remember feeling the same when a friendship ended," "I was careless about what I said to Joe," and "I felt this same way when I said the wrong thing to Mindy and she turned her back on me.")

4. Note which of the associations seems most painful, and then identify areas of which you want to be more aware in the future. (Example: "I was curt with a committee member in my e-mails. I could lose the connection with him in an instant.")

5. Choose an action based on your association that would also honor the energy of the dream. (Example: "I choose to be more

careful in my transactions, especially with e-mails, which can turn others off very quickly.")

6. Allow yourself to bring the insight from your dream forward by making associations with its theme in your daytime awareness. (Example: Rereading all e-mails before sending them, and waiting a day to do so, especially if the issue is sticky or complex.)

7. Notice the effects of the action in your life. Notice if the dream recurs to remind you there is more to do. If you have made a positive decision related to the intended message from the subconscious mind, the dream will most likely not recur.

Creating a Place of Beauty for Yourself

Having found a safe, appropriate place for your inner critic, you are now ready to do something spontaneous. Remember, nothing is required except a willingness to enjoy the moment.

One possibility is simply to rearrange several objects from your home. You might do it just for the sheer pleasure of seeing different shapes and colors come together. Creating beauty with symbols, words, pictures, rhythms, aromas, tastes, and music is innately satisfying. The more senses you involve the better. As children, we probably made special areas for play—houses, tents, and caves—quite naturally. I now delight in watching my grandchildren bring together rocks and plants to make their "gardens" or "hideouts."

Having a specific purpose in mind is also a possibility. You can make it a celebration. You can remind yourself of a good adventure, remember a friend who is no longer with you, recall a special day, relieve the tension from a traumatic event, or make a place of meditation and peace.

Spontaneous expressions about traumatic loss have come to be respected as a necessary component of grieving. We often see markers, flowers, candles, photos, balloons, or little gifts at roadsides near the site of a fatal accident. Some become mini-parks and gathering places for loved ones. I recently saw a marker for a wilderness trail guide killed in a car accident that consisted of hiking sticks, water bottles, trail mix, and other essential gear. It was touching to see the care with which fellow hikers honored their fallen friend.

The human need to express concern and to feel connection with others forces us to invent new structures. You may want to add an idea from this exercise to your own continued processing of a significant event.

Exercise 10.4 Making a Spontaneous Object Arrangement

1. Select five to seven objects, of different sizes, from your home that either attract you or have special meaning for you.

2. Find a cloth or piece of colored paper that can serve as a background or base.

3. Place the objects on the background material and move them around into the configuration you like best.

4. Add any other objects that seem to complement what you have so far. You might also add a food item, musical instrument, flower, word, poem, or scent.

5. When you feel complete, allow yourself to rest and appreciate what came together for you. Then and only then, allow your more objective self to review what you have done and note how you feel.

Many people find this kind of activity to be a visual reminder of inner, intuitive processing. Karen filled her apartment with many arrangements with personal meanings. She observed, "It's like being greeted by friends when I look at them. Even though I live alone, I feel surrounded by others' good wishes." With a little play from her intuition, she created an environment to overcome loneliness.

****

Actively inviting inner wisdom helps build a deep sense of satisfaction. It allows glimpses of hope and joy in times when our lives might slip into fear or helplessness.

Chapter Eleven
The Divine Spark Within

A person is neither a thing nor a process, but an opening or clearing through which the Absolute can manifest.
—Martin Heidegger

As we trust and honor the truths within ourselves, we come to value the divine spark residing in each person. Each person seems to be an embodied aspect of a much larger unity. As we seek ways of understanding the meaning and purpose of our lives, we also stretch awareness to greater than personal dimensions, into the *transpersonal* realms.

When we perceive ourselves as energy beings living in a temporary human lifetime, we begin to catch glimpses of the ongoing nature of consciousness. Many of us have had the experience of feeling deep connections with others who live at a distance or are no longer physically alive. Energetic bonds appear to be timeless and beyond our limited understandings. Even personal physical death can be viewed as a transition, a prelude to a wider dream as imaginative as we wish for it to be.

The transpersonal is defined as across, through, and beyond the personal self. Exploring this domain takes our understandings of creativity and health to another level. As we explore the mysteries of life on this planet, we come face to face with the unlimited supply of

Energy evident in our universe. The awe experienced in the wonders of nature is so deeply ingrained in humanity that it has been known throughout the ages by thousands of names, including: Creative Mind, Source, All That Is, Higher Power, Unifying Force, Allah, the One with a thousand names, the Ground of Being, the Absolute, the Unknowable, the Unamed, Intelligent Design, Oneness, or Good Orderly Direction (one of many God acronyms).

The transpersonal is not defined by social or religious affiliations; instead, it is a reflection of the individual's quest for finding a place of meaning in the vast universe. Everyone is basically spiritual. Spirituality manifests in different forms, depending on maturity and insight. For a young person, the concept of an external God resembling a parent may be easiest to grasp. Later in life, one becomes more conscious of seeing God in all living things, the web of life. This perception activates social concern to protect community life and the environment. Through activity on behalf of others and altruism one learns to honor the divinity within oneself. Creation with all its possibilities is the affirmation of intelligent consciousness intrinsic to the web of life. As author David Korten writes in *The Great Turning,* "[This] model suggests a living cosmos that continues to grow and evolve as the eternal Spirit continuously manifests itself by vibrating Creation into existence in a manner suggestive of the ways in which quantum physics describes material reality."[1]

The Ground of Being is evident in every person, creature, or particle. We are in constant relationship with this Spirit and have no existence separate from it. Our place in the living cosmos is one of helping to bring about, to cocreate, a world in alignment with Spirit. Fear in this context is a temporary disconnection from Spirit, when we've forgotten our home and intention. Further, sin is seen not as a transgression of an external set of rules but rather as a betrayal of Spirit. Self-centeredness, greed, or violence are destructive because they separate us from our spiritual Source. When we are in harmony in our relation to Spirit, we are in sync with ourselves, our environments, relationships, and planetary responsibilities. In addition, fascinating synchronicities seem to appear when we align with spirituality and sense of purpose.

Defining ourselves as energy-filled, spiritual beings in a world full of uncertainties is perhaps the most creative endeavor to which we can aspire—it requires a leap into the unknown. Connecting with the Ground of Being opens doors not only to trusting personal intuition, but also to sensing Guidance. It allows us to reach unlimited potentials. It widens curiosity about the future and supports us in facing perils. It informs our path even when we have no idea where we are going with a new direction or event.

Be Careful about Your Beliefs

For those who limit their beliefs to seeing God as an external parent, belief about the emotional disposition of the parent brings powerful consequences. Gail Ironson studied the effects of religious beliefs on measurable immune system factors in patients with HIV. In one of the first studies to link particular beliefs with immune system changes, she showed that predictors of disease progression in those who viewed God as a punishing, judging authority differed from predictors in those who believed in a benevolent, forgiving God. She concludes, "This one item [believing in a punishing deity] is related to an increased likelihood that the patient will develop an opportunistic infection or die. These beliefs predict disease progression even more strongly than depression."[2]

The quest for spiritual connectedness is highly individualized, as unique as your fingerprints or energetic blueprint. The still prevailing mechanistic view of a clock-like universe governed by a punishing God stands in sharp contrast to the living spirituality of harmony with all of nature. Even though the forces of the universe remain mostly unknowable to our finite minds, they appear to be inherently benevolent. If we align with trust in basic goodwill, it is quite likely we will enhance patterns of gene expression that allow DNA to align with positive health and well-being.

Author, publisher, and energy psychology practitioner Dawson Church reports recent HeartMath experiments in which human placental DNA was measured in relation to an individual's intention to either wind the molecular strands more tightly or to allow them to loosen. Loosening the strand makes gene expression more likely. While holding feelings of love and appreciation, participants were able to change DNA conformations as measured by the molecule's absorption of ultraviolet light.[3] Positive emotions, including basic understanding of the universe as kindly, generate coherence between heart rhythms and influence gene expression and upregulation of the immune system. When anger, frustration, or anxiety are present in the person, no gene expression occurs or there may be downregulation of the genes that would support immune function as measured in mature lymphophyte formation.[4]

Aligning with a benevolent force greater than us is not only more in harmony with the realities of our natural world, it also is a strong factor in optimal aging, creativity, and health. Prayer is, in its broadest sense, the setting of our focused intention to invite the world to manifest in beneficent ways. It is good medicine for the person praying as well as the receiver. A meta-study summarizes more than twelve hundred scientific studies of prayer and shows the link between prayerful intention, health, and longevity.[5] Other studies show regular acts of altruism prolong lives and improve happiness.[6] Among those who practice a strong faith and help others, stronger overall health is evidenced.

Hug Trees Often

Connecting with nature brings us into a state of psychoenergetic harmony and connects us with the creative energy of the world. The word "nature" stems from *natus,* Latin for "birth." It is in our human temperament to be born and reborn when we connect with our natural surroundings.

For many urban dwellers, there is significant disconnection from nature. Lisa told me she was afraid of being outdoors. For many years her world consisted of living in her apartment, getting into her car to shop and visit, and then returning home. Although she was only fifty-three years old, her life was more like that of someone over a hundred. Part of her healing was learning to sit outside my office just to enjoy colors of grasses and trees. We used energetic maneuvers to release her fears and install a sense of safety. She later delighted in finding the holes made by underground animals, something she had never noticed before. The warmth of the sun nurtured her more than any recollections of her dysfunctional parents. Lisa found peace and satisfaction by just learning to sit outside with me for an hour.

Intentionally choosing to experience nature is deeply rewarding and gives opportunity for self-nurturing and comfort. In the computer age, most people need encouragement to fully see, listen, and interact with their surroundings. As we notice how simple and complex forms are interwoven into fascinating patterns all around us, we develop appreciation for Creative Mind, the imagined unifying force in the order of nature.

The suggestions in the following exercise are starting places for strengthening your connection to Spirit.

Exercise 11.1 Increasing Your Enjoyment of Nature

1. Think about a recent time you were outside. What did you notice? What pleased you? What comforted you? What surprised you? Enjoy recalling as many details as possible.

2. What did you have to do to make sure you had the time? What would you need to do to make sure you have such a time again? Set your intention to make time for enjoying the comforts and surprises of the outdoors.

3. Take a walk outside for ten minutes or so in silence. Allow your-self to notice all the colors you see, hear all the sounds around you, and sense the textures of various objects. Close your eyes and just enjoy the moment. Write down any words or ideas com-ing to you.

4. Hug a tree. Touch the earth. Notice how healthy energy moves within you while breathing fully, in and out. Now shake, stretch, skip, and bounce to release any stagnation or blockage from your body and mind.

Gratitude—The Gift That Keeps On Giving

Living with gratitude is free. It costs nothing but a slight shift in consciousness. Instead of looking at what one does not have, or what is lacking, we bring our focus to what we do have, and how we are blessed. The sense of gratefulness enriches our sense of joy and generativity. Thankfulness also permits us to see the world around us with increased sensitivity.

Exercise 11.2 Expanding Gratitude from the Heart Center

1. Think of the four directions of the sun. Stand in a favorite place of your home, or imagine being there. Align to the four direc-tions of the sun as if you were a compass.

2. Think of someone who loves and supports you unconditionally. Step into the direction of the compass to face this person across the miles; extend your good wishes from your heart center to him or her. Let warm feelings radiate from your heart like a con-necting rainbow or the expanding sound of a bell.

3. Think of other loved ones and let your heart center open and expand as you send your caring wishes in a similar manner in all four compass directions.

4. List five people or things for which you are grateful. Now name five more. Note how gratefulness builds on itself. Notice how you feel as you step into the vibration of appreciation.

The Big Qi

As we become more aware of our own vital life force or *qi*, we see a world filled with energy. Our sun, with its vast, ongoing dynamic of fusion from hydrogen to helium, radiates the warmth and light that make life possible on Earth. Even this vibrant solar energy is only a small sampling of the seemingly unlimited energies that fueled the "big bang" and started our universe on its present path over thirteen billion years ago. The canopy of stars on a clear night shows the light of billions of suns and a vast array of galaxies beyond our Milky Way. Whether we believe in a personal God or not, we can be filled with a sense of wonder as we contemplate the Energy present in our universe.

The vital life force within is a personalized reflection of this Great *Qi*. Personal energy thrives in the presence of the sun. For many people, deprivation of sunlight is the cause of depression, lethargy, apathy, and other forms of emotional disturbance. Seasonal affective disorder (SAD) is becoming more clearly understood as the emotional response to light deprivation in late autumn and winter by a significant portion of the population. Regular daily treatment with exposure to full-spectrum lighting, resembling the vibrations of the sun's rays, has been found to alleviate many of SAD's symptoms.

Many people notice shifts in emotional states on rainy or cloudy days. It appears that our systems require inflow of more qi at those times. Because we have our own imaginations and energy systems with which to work, we don't need to buy full-spectrum light bulbs to treat ourselves. Here are two exercises that allow you to bring more qi into your own body and energy system by aligning with the limitless supply of energy in the universe.

Exercise 11.3 Bringing Solar Energy to the Chakras and Biofield

1. Stand outside facing the sun and stretch your arms as far back as they will comfortably go.

Bringing Solar Energy to the Chakras and Biofield.

2. Feel the warmth of the sun on your arms and bring it in to your heart center (mid-chest) and solar plexus (upper mid-abdomen) with repeated sweeping motions. Take several deep breaths.

3. As an alternative on a cloudy day, or if you're indoors, imagine the radiant light of the sun and bring it in with big sweeping motions. Notice how the energy shifts within you as you breathe deeply and image the presence of sunlight.

4. While either standing in the sun or imagining it, bring the warmth and light of the sun into each of your seven energy centers, starting at the base of your spine (see figure 3.3). You may also want to add an affirmation as you bring your hands over each chakra and think of its function.

    Root chakra: "I support and nurture my aliveness, my right to be fully present in my body."

    Sacral chakra: " I honor my feelings, my ability to choose to keep what fits for me, and to release what does not."

    Solar plexus: "I recognize my ability to think clearly, to make decisions, and to be effectively assertive."

Heart chakra: "I radiate caring and goodwill to all around me, I forgive easily, and I accept myself unconditionally."

Throat chakra: "I express my being easily through sound, words, writing, and other creative means."

Brow chakra: "I see with insight, intuition, and compassion; I speak my truth."

Crown chakra: "I align my being with sunlight and the wonder of the universal energy flow."

5. Feel your whole body filling with nourishing sunlight. Let it flow to every cell in your body. Sense sunlight warming each of your internal organs and bring your hands to any part of the body needing extra warmth.

6. Feel your entire biofield expanding with the inflow of sunlight. Stretch your arms as wide as you can reach in all directions to sense the fullness of your being.

Exercise 11.4 Bringing Solar Energy to the Acupoints

1. Use the breath to release any pressure or tension.

2. Then tap or hold the fourteen acupoints (see figure 3.5) while either standing in the sun or imaging radiant, powerful sunlight. As you tap each point (eyebrow, side of eye, under eye, under nose, under lip, collarbone, under arm, lower rib cage, inside of thumb, index, middle, and small fingers, side of hand, and between the last two knuckles), feel your body awaken to aliveness.

3. As you tap each point, you may add an attunement phrase, such as "Bringing in the unlimited supply of *qi*" or "Aligning with solar energy and strength." Notice any tingling or vibrancy in your body after you finish.

Connecting with the Higher Self

The playfulness and generativity so apparent in nature connects us with unexpected and surprising parts of ourselves. In effect, we realize, "I am so much more than my problems, my history, my family legacy, even my long-term patterns and beliefs." We recognize there is a transpersonal quality within us that goes beyond our day-to-day struggles, something we call our higher Self. This quality can be accessed through intention and can greatly enhance inner vitality.

Connecting with our higher Self acknowledges the spark of personal consciousness reflected in the whole universe and its divine order. The higher Self is characterized by wisdom and nurturing; it recognizes our journey through our life stages without getting bogged down in details. As we learn to trust intuition, wisdom emerges and we begin to see new possibilities for ourselves.

Here is a suggestion for connecting with this wiser part of yourself. You might also think of this exercise as a means for accessing guidance.

Exercise 11.5 Dialogue with Your Higher Self

1. After centering with the breath, allow your mind to wander to a big question you have for yourself. (Examples: "What is my best course of action for my future?" or "How can I most effectively be of service during my life?") Write your question down.

2. Take several deep breaths and allow your consciousness to lift higher. See yourself and your particular life stage with acceptance, free of judgments or criticism.

3. Restate the question, and write down as many thoughts as come to you quickly regarding your question.

4. Anytime the flow stops, ask, "Is there anything else?" Trust that there is a wiser aspect of you that can come in with the next breath.

5. Notice any particular voice or image associated with the messages you receive. Some people get a sense of an animal, a loved one, an angel, or a spirit guide, but it is not required. Just enjoy what comes to you from the deeper and higher aspects of yourself.

6. When you get a sense that what you've received is complete, extend thankfulness. Appreciate how there is always more to learn from your inner being, your own best friend.

7. Gently come back to full awareness, feeling connection with the breath, and then read what came to you.

Creativity Flows from Ultimate Qi

We may speak of our Higher Power as a personal presence or as a transcendent quality of the universal *qi*. Either way, the transpersonal allows us to extend the sense of the possible and to reach new potentials. Visual artist Julia Cameron connects creativity with human energy in this way: "Creativity is God energy flowing through us, shaped by us, like light flowing through a crystal prism. When we are clear about who we are and what we are doing, the energy flows freely and we experience no strain."[7]

Those who allow themselves to be filled with inner light as they align with their life purpose shine forth in wonder-full ways. Some shine brightly throughout history as social leaders, composers of music, poets, or expressive artists. Others become hidden treasures to their communities of family and friends, a blessing to all whose lives they touch. When we align with our sense of purpose and guiding direction, we have increased personal satisfaction; we bring inspiration to ourselves and, through this, to loved ones and others.

We begin to see how we are part of a vast integration much larger than the sum of separate parts. Our work in the world is a form of cocreation in which we participate with the ultimate *qi*. As we align our individual energies with Creative Mind, we become enriched and insights flow.

All truly creative people have a profound sense of humility around what they are able to bring forth through their alignment with Source. Edgar Cayce, the "sleeping prophet" who gave thousands of insightful readings for others on health and life patterns, always spoke simply of sharing what he read in the records on the higher planes of awareness. Psychologist Carl Jung spoke of tapping into the collective unconscious, the wide stream uniting all of humankind. He saw individual consciousness as part of a much larger, integrated whole.

Great musicians and poets throughout the ages speak of writing down what they hear on the higher planes, rather than take sole credit for their compositions. Most creative people speak of being inspired by nature, the seasons, the discoveries advanced by science, or the wondrous complexity of our world. There seems to be a direct and acknowledged lineage from writers, artists, and composers to their Higher Power. The greater the vision of this Source, the more inspiring the message will be.

In music especially, the sense of cocreation is continuous. The composer cocreates and unites with Source while putting down the notes. Next the performing artists participate in the energy of the composition as they connect with the intent of the composer. And finally, listeners are cocreators in experiencing the music and letting its message touch their souls.

"Papa" Franz Joseph Haydn, "father" of the string quartet and composer of more than a hundred symphonies, was unabashedly connected to Divine Energy when he expressed his muse. He wrote in his journals, "When I think upon God, my heart is so full of joy that the notes dance and leap, as it were, from my pen, and since God has given me a cheerful heart it will be pardoned me that I serve Him with a cheerful spirit."[8] To this day, musicians and listeners who hear Haydn's works, enjoy the pervading sense of happiness and joy that emanated from this man's soul.

We need to find ways of lifting beyond ordinary perceptions to higher levels of consciousness. We start by recognizing that we are capable of sensing subtle energies beyond our cognitions or physical senses. We move to higher sense perceptions by paying attention to the spaces between our thoughts. We increase awareness of the constant interplay of light and shadow, noting shifts from order to disorder, and then back to new forms of order. As we contemplate our wondrous world, we can become the opening through which the Absolute can manifest.

Some may fear stepping into uncharted territories. In this exercise, you will learn a practical, grounded way to extend your consciousness to the transpersonal realm.

Exercise 11.6 Lifting to Higher Planes of Awareness

1. Feel the breath as connection between your body, mind, and spirit. Sense your connection to the earth through your feet and at the base of the spine.

2. With each in-breath, allow a sense of the Infinite to come to you via sky, trees, and mountains. Continue to release the breath as you bring in more and more *qi*.

3. Let your consciousness reach to a cloud and then move above the cloud. Move higher than all the clouds as you feel the support of your steady breath. Imagine stretching to the horizon of visible blue sky and then go beyond it to the deep indigo blue of space.

4. Allow yourself to sense fine shadings of color beyond ordinary seeing; let yourself hear sounds that might reflect the movements of the planets and the stars, the "'harmony of the spheres" described by Greek philosophers. Sense the safety of journeying beyond usual ways of thinking by feeling the connecting breath.

5. Imagine you are a space traveler who is safely able to explore the higher planes of the cosmos. This may take you to the outer planes of miniscule vibrating strings of energy or to the inner planes of connecting with loved ones.

6. Take in as many details as you can of these subtle planes while still sensing the comfort of the breath. Gently let yourself return to your starting place, while continuing to hold the images or concepts that came to you.

7. Draw a quick sketch of what you saw, or describe it in words. Honor whatever you received, even the slightest trace of an image. Give thanks to your inner being and ongoing guidance.

Enthusiasm literally means to be filled with divine inspiration. As we experience the quality of enthusiasm supported by the unlimited energy of the cosmos, we come to express our deepest feelings. Such deeply felt emotions may begin to sound like a rhythm, a melody, a series of words, or a poem; they may translate into pictures, colors, shapes, forms, or symbols; they may be sensed as textures, three-dimensional objects, or turn into dancing movements. As you live with enthusiasm and a sense of your Higher Power, you empower confidence to express your unique gifts and talents.

****

The concepts and exercises given in this chapter suggest that life artistry is related to willingness to trust in a friendly, transpersonal universe. More intelligence, compassion, and caring are available to us than we can fully comprehend with finite minds. The willingness to hold faith is the generative power behind a fulfilled life. It is the supportive energy for becoming the creative artist of your life.

Chapter Twelve
Trusting in the Resilience of Hope

Hope is the thing with feathers
That perches in the soul,
And sings the tune without the words
And never stops at all.
—Emily Dickinson

A Native American tradition teaches that there are two plans for every day: the plan set by each individual and the plan of Mystery. Both plans create the interplay of life events. Our lives can become easier when we incorporate a transpersonal perspective, a sense of confidence in benevolent mysterious forces greater than us and our knowing. Although we carefully accept personal responsibility for our choices, we also recognize how much is not within our power to control or change. "Thy will, not my will, be done" is the prayer of trust and hope.

As we face realities such as illness, physical limitations, or a diminishing circle of friends, we explore all possible avenues to lessen emotional distress or pain. When we have done all we can within human capabilities, we should be open to turning things over to Higher Power. It's vital to know we can ask for help with heartfelt prayer.

A transpersonal and open-ended life philosophy augments resources for healing. Multidimensional healing is always possible, even in the face of devastating loss, incurable illness, long-term pain, the challenges of aging, and the inevitable end of life. This broad concept of bringing healing to all possible dimensions of the energy system—physical, emotional, mental, or spiritual—nourishes hope. In spite of adversity, there appears to be an unstoppable human capacity for inner strength and faith.

Recent publications emphasize the power of such positive attributes as resilience and hope. There are dynamic energy resources for bringing positive confidence to even the most devastating experiences. Throughout the ages, mystics have called life's great challenges that bring one to the brink of despair "the dark night of the soul." As we work our way through such perils, we can discover heretofore-unknown resources and inner strengths.

Keeping Hope Alive

People can live without food for several weeks. They can live without water for a few days. Without hope, however, an individual may not live more than a few minutes, especially when that person has suicidal thoughts and available opportunity. Hope is the essential ingredient for a quality life. Hope is the essential quality each soul must maintain in order to nurture self and others.

Positive psychologist Martin Seligman has studied the effects of cancer patients' attitudes over many years. He found that those with an attitude of "positive expectancy" actually lived longer and with greater enjoyment than those who saw themselves as victims, succumbing to what he called "learned helplessness."[1] As we come to understand the magic of genetic expression, it makes sense that attitudes influence our quality of life, capacity for enjoyment, and immune system function. The decision to see ourselves as helpless, a victim of fate, may, at first, appear to be a safe choice: We can be passive and do nothing. A "victim stance" may even engender others' sympathy or pity and absolve us from personal responsibility. But loss of hope is the most damaging loss to the human psyche because it takes away our sense of direction and meaning. Our very humanness resides in the indomitable capacity for hope.

Mental attitude is the ultimate powerful choice within every life situation. Before Mattie Stepanek died at age eleven, he had become a well-known poet who made many TV appearances. Three of his siblings had died from a rare form of mitochondrial myopathy and Mattie had the same disorder, being kept alive by a tracheostomy, a ventilator, and oxygen. His writing was simple and direct: "Whoever I am, and whatever happens, / I will always love my body and mind, / even if it has different abilities / than other peoples' bodies and minds. / I will always be happy, because / I will always be me."[2]

Mattie's unaffected wisdom brings a profound message of hope. By comparison, most daily lives have relatively minor setbacks. Nevertheless, the quality of hope needs daily renewal, and we must surround ourselves with inspirational ideas and positive social environments. Even the media, so very prone to reporting mayhem in great detail, are always looking for messages of hope. Through heroes like Mattie, they recognize profound human interest and popular appeal.

We come to decision points that endorse either paths of hope or those of despair. We ask ourselves: Is life an adventure or a meaningless exercise? Shall we take responsibility or blame others? Shall we access or ignore inner healing potentials? Shall we actively counteract or give in to negative thinking? Shall we find ways to express ourselves and our intensely felt emotions? Or hold back and give up?

These ongoing decisions impact us profoundly, even when they are outside our awareness. In any given moment, we have the opportunity to clearly understand hope and its accompanying resilience.

Taking Responsibility versus Blaming

Blaming others for personal distress is all too easy. When considering fragmented families and generational wounds, friends or counselors must beware of falling into the trap of placing blame elsewhere. It's very easy to see another's pain as injustice, rather than as an opportunity for further learning. Helpers must be careful to frame their point of view from the perspective of hope so that it can be understood by the person caught up in blaming others.

In whatever way befits the circumstances, we need to ask, "What can you harvest in understanding from the situation you told me about?" You may be giving the person an opportunity to look at things in a new light. Of course, any intervention has to be totally free of judgment or any sense of "I told you so."

Acknowledging feelings of anger or discouragement are good starting places for assuming personal responsibility. The exercise of rubbing the tender spot on the upper left chest while stating a feeling, such as "Even though I have intense anger about ____, I still deeply and profoundly accept myself," is an active way of acknowledging what exists without giving away personal power. Gradually, we can stop wishing others would change to suit our wishes and come to appreciate our own strengths and abilities. Appropriate self-responsibility also opens the door to new thinking about long-term goals and taking charge of one's life.

Minnie's Story: Alienation by an Adult Child

After a long and difficult relationship, Minnie's daughter wrote a letter cutting off all communication for an unspecified period of time. Perhaps because of increased dispersion of families over long distances, "alienation by adult children" has become much more common in recent years and is a painful, hidden secret held by many parents in later life. An additional dilemma is that visitation with grandchildren often terminates with such estrangement.

Minnie sobbed and expressed her anger and despair to her neighbor. Tessa listened quietly as Minnie wailed, "How could my daughter do this? I tried my best with her through all the teenage years and the disaster of her marriages. Her children are my only solace. Now she's taken them away from me as well. She's a failure! I'm furious! I'm taking her out of my will!"

Tessa was sorely tempted to agree and join in with Minnie. After thinking what would be best, she offered, "You are still you despite what has happened. I care for you; you have many friends. Let's explore what you could learn about yourself or your daughter from this painful situation." Careful to make 90 percent of the communication positive and caring, she maintained an opening for further dialogue.

Minnie was taken aback by Tessa's reflection until she understood it in a more positive light. Several days later, she asked, "What would you do in my shoes?" The friends came to agree that a counselor at the community center might be a helpful resource. With adequate supportive help, Minnie then found ways of nurturing herself.

It took four years before her daughter was ready to lift the "ban" and reopen communications. In the meantime, Minnie learned how to avoid some of the most obvious relationship pitfalls.

Connecting with Personal Energy Resources versus Ignoring the Inner Healer

Self-healing capacities reside within our psychoenergetic systems. By making alliances with our energy resources, we can experience the joy of discovery, release of tension, and inflow of new options. Whole new dimensions of self-understanding open up as we envision and work with the meridian acupoints, the major chakras, and the luminous biofield.

Ignoring inner healing and self-regulating potentials leaves us empty and at the mercy of whatever comes our way. Energy-based resources, such as quickly releasing stress, developing methods for trusting intuition, and finding effective dialogue with our higher Self, give us practical tools for self-empowerment. The moment we remember our personal energy system, we increase our self-efficacy, abandon "learned helplessness," and move into a vibration of "positive expectancy."

Actively Seeking Relief from Negativity versus Giving In

While acknowledging realistic discouragement, we can still hold on to our sense of inner strength and power. Victor Frankl, a Viennese psychiatrist who spent four harsh, dehumanizing years in Nazi concentration camps, emerged to teach messages of hope for the rest of his life. His message was that no matter how desperate our situation, as creative human beings, we have the right to choose our internal attitude. He reflected about his experiences, "Every day, every hour offered the opportunity to make a decision, a decision which determined whether you would or would not submit to those powers which threatened to rob you of your very self, your inner freedom; which determined whether or not you would become the plaything of circumstance, renouncing freedom and dignity to become molded into the form of the typical inmate...Man does not simply exist but always decides what his existence will be, what he will become in the next moment."[3]

Frankl saw some of the prisoners remaining steadfast in their dignity and humanity. They gave comfort to others and shared even their last pieces of bread. He also observed camp prisoners who gave in to negative thinking and died rapidly. Often, these deaths occurred after a meaningful anniversary. The prisoner would say, "If I'm not out of here by my birthday, I will give up." Such thoughts quickly became self-fulfilling prophecies.

Living in hope, especially in adverse circumstances, requires incredible courage. Hope generates resilience, the ability to bounce back from difficulties while neither ignoring nor being engulfed by them. Accessing the creative energy of our lives requires tenacity and willingness to postpone immediate gratification in favor of future outcomes. Despite glossy portrayals in movies and on television, success does not usually come instantly, or in a sixty-minute time-frame. It comes from repeatedly learning and working at something. Energetic approaches support such perseverance through readily accessible daily exercises and increased sense of empowerment.

Joyce's Story: Overcoming Fear

Joyce was a volunteer in a charitable organization. While its director was often emotionally abusive, the thought of finding a different placement totally overwhelmed Joyce with fear. Feeling stuck in a hopeless situation, Joyce needed to take responsibility for her own feelings rather than passively wishing the director would change. Joyce learned to address her fear with a mantra acknowledging reality: "Even though I am afraid of volunteering in a different place, I deeply and profoundly accept myself." She also used acupoint tapping to diminish her fear. She then went through strength-building exercises including listing skills and writing a resume. Her persistence paid off. Recognizing she was free to make new choices at whatever time was right for her, she found volunteer listings that corresponded to her skills.

As Joyce's self-confidence increased, much of the abuse seemed to decrease as well at the center. It was as if the grumpy director saw Joyce in a different light when her self-perceptions changed. Instead of giving in to a sense of helplessness, Joyce ventured into positive expectancy, listened to her heart, and started living with boldness and courage. The word "courage" literally means "taking heart."

Seeking Self-Expression versus Holding Back

Expressing ourselves through music, dance, writing, gardening, or painting is not just decorative—it is life-giving and hope-generating. Our souls need outlets for expression. All that is required is the willingness to begin, and to persist. Allowing ourselves to flow is necessary to counterbalance the many demands on our time.

Holding back from generative impulses takes a great deal of energy. Think of activities you have persistently put off, such as exercising, taking a walk, or writing a note. How many times have you thought about them only to push the idea aside? Consider the number of times you have postponed an activity and you might recognize how much time and attention was consumed by holding yourself back. Quite possibly it was equivalent to the amount of time the actual activity would have taken!

Notice also what happens when you finally begin a postponed activity. My experience has been one of tremendous relief and renewed emotional energy. While the mind might still think about what it was trying to put off, you can cheerfully say, "Well, I just did it!" Gradually, the hard work of procrastinating and avoiding is replaced by satisfactions. Hanging on to old patterns is tedious—and quite unnecessary.

Turning Pottery Flaws into Beauty

Generating opportunities for self-expression flows easily when we pay attention to our surroundings and follow intuition. Suzanne Hermes was a program volunteer counselor with high-risk groups on a Navajo reservation. Feeling dispossessed by losing their land and traditions, many of the Native Americans had fallen into drug and alcohol abuse and hopeless suicidal behaviors. Some had brain damage from severe accidents. Talk therapy had little meaning for treating their profound "loss of soul." As she encouraged group expression through drawing, sand painting, and shield making in the Navajo tradition, Suzanne discovered that simple art-making engendered a transfusion of hope. "Imagination is a survival tool," she observed, "just as play can be. In letting the mind go in nondestructive ways of being, we can thrive, survive, and experience joy and reverie."[4]

With the power of her vision, Suzanne generated funding for group therapy that incorporated expressive art-making. Over time, the pottery, which included images of the clan and guardian animals, became transformative symbols. The participants started coming up with new ideas. They turned flaws and imperfections in the ceramics into something new and stunning. Their ancestral heritage was steeped in the tradition of walking the path of beauty in harmony with self and others. Thus making objects of beauty supported spiritual connection with their lineage and brought it to life in the present. After describing his terrible life prior to involvement with the community arts project, one of the most severely traumatized participants tearfully concluded, "Against all odds, I now walk in beauty."

Self-expressive activity, in whatever chosen medium, has redeeming qualities for the human soul. Through creativity, our consciousness is enlarged. We connect with our collective human heritage. Links to the distant past and ancestors live in the subconscious mind. As we bring those sensitivities into the present, transcendence becomes possible. We can walk in beauty, in harmony and with a sense of pride.

Listening within and redirecting thinking with repeated thoughts or a mantra is very helpful for accessing full human potential. A well-known Buddhist meditation I have adapted for clients' needs engenders positive expectancy.

Exercise 12.1 Hopefulness Meditation

1. Allow yourself a quiet time without interruption for ten to fifteen minutes in a comfortable place. Exhale fully while releasing any tension or stress.

2. While holding your hands in turn over each chakra, starting at the base (see figure 3.3), sense your seven energy centers and how they support your wholeness and well-being.

3. While maintaining a steady inflow and outflow of your breath, allow yourself to repeat the following thought patterns several times:

- May I be filled with lovingkindness.

- May I be peaceful and content.

- May I release any burdens from the past.

- May I be joyous. May I be healthy.

Repeat these thoughts until they come to you without effort.

4. Now allow yourself to think of someone with whom you have had difficulty communicating. See the person and extend your caring thoughts to him or her:

    - May you be filled with lovingkindness.

    - May you be peaceful and content.

    - May you release the burdens of the past.

    - May you be joyous. May you be healthy.

    Repeat until you see the person surrounded with healing light and you can look without pain at the person.

5. Over time, you may notice the power of this message to yourself and to the other person. You are not helpless; your thoughts and intentions have an energy that can be actively directed to assist yourself and others.

6. Take the final moment of this quiet time to acknowledge your many gifts and to thank yourself for honoring inner wisdom.

Ted's Story: Persistence of Hope

Ted's son lost the right to shared custody of his oldest child, Ted's grandson. The child's mother had moved to another state and complex legal maneuvering followed. Ted felt the loss of access to his grandchildren very deeply. He often blamed his new wife and himself for not doing enough to stop the legal processes. Years later, when the grandson turned eighteen and was ready for college, there was the opportunity to renew the relationship. Trying to work out eight years of separation from each other would take time and tough determination on both sides. Ted felt hopeless and helpless, especially since the grandson's natural interests now focused on peer relationships and college plans.

After giving Ted plenty of room to vent his frustrations, I suggested the hopefulness meditation. The repeated phrases helped him feel calmer. As his attention shifted to sending his grandson light and caring, he felt warmth and a sense of connection. He repeated this practice many times. Later, when Ted and his grandson finally reconnected at a large family reunion, Ted told him about it. It was a special moment for both of them when Ted shared his active reaching out with caring intention.

Opening to Full Human Potential

The guiding prayer of Alcoholics Anonymous is "God grant me the serenity to accept the things I cannot change, courage to change the things I can, and wisdom to know the difference." Realizing what we can and cannot do in any given situation is crucial. It is sacred work to know when we have done all we can and to turn matters over to Higher Power. Connection to the spiritual dimension assists us in moving beyond our human limitations.

Living in hope engenders creativity and originality. These qualities become constricted or very limited when we are stressed. Full potential becomes possible when inner balance is restored and becomes actualized when we consciously choose to express inner wisdom. The outcome may simply be enjoying life more, taking time to connect with nature, or developing deeper spiritual connections. Full-energy living means seeking an ongoing journey toward wholeness and healing despite setbacks.

A conceptual model of the ongoing healing process may be helpful here. It incorporates releasing distress and moving forward to generate new choices, connections, images, symbols, meaning, and a sense of flow. Figure 12.1 is a schematic of such an ongoing dynamic.

Releasing → Accessing → Generating → Imagining → Finding → Enjoying
distress   new choices   connections   possibilities   meaning   flow!!!

Figure 12.1. The Healing Continuum.

As we can see, the dynamic for full-energy living is not limited to problem solving or finding pleasure. It reflects daily choices of letting go of an identified distress or emotional state by refocusing with balancing, releasing limiting beliefs, and treating specific issues with self-help patterns. As we integrate learning and diminish personal distress, we are able to install empowering beliefs, enjoy more creativity, and participate in ever-expanding self-awareness. The connecting line with the arrow and movement from left to right in figure 12.1 suggests this work can happen quickly. You might accomplish this with a single intentional movement, one of the exercises in this book, or spin of the entire body to release stagnation or blockage. And you can repeat the combination of patterns that work for you as often as necessary.

****

Social scientist and philosopher Michael Lerner captures the essence of hope's message in this way: "Energy always flows toward hope, community, love, generosity, mutual recognition, and spiritual aliveness…or it flows toward despair, cynicism, fear that there is not enough, paranoia about the intentions of others, and a desire to control."[5] The ninety million Americans who are currently over fifty-five years of age have untold opportunities to choose the energy pattern they wish.

Today we can experience hope's fresh perceptions, hold hope for a second chance at healing our relationships, and participate in an ongoing process of recreating ourselves and our lives. We can continue our lifelong expansion into unlimited potentials with the trusted ally of hope.

Part IV:
Energy Resources for Special Needs

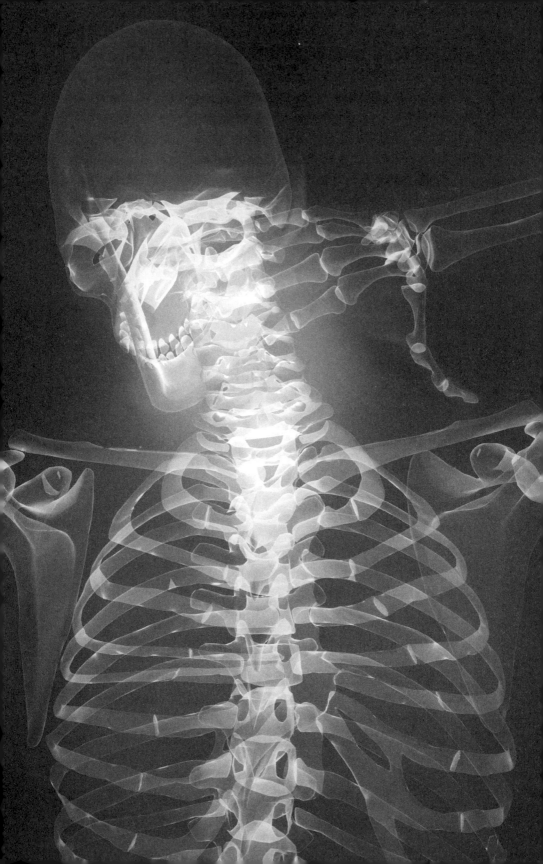

Chapter Thirteen
A New Look at Pain

According to Buddhism, there is no personal self.
If that is so, then whose arthritis is this?
—Jewish wisdom and humor

[H]ealing our suffering means not so much the absence of pain but the ability
to meet it with love and compassion instead of blame, fear, and loathing.
—Stephen Levine

How Is Pain Useful?

As people mature chronologically, many begin to notice aches and pains in parts of the body never noticed before. Some take affront when they find the body is no longer willing or able to do what the mind wishes. Many regard physical pain as an unwelcome distraction. Still others become so obsessed with pain they live in fear of every new sensation. Conversations about body failings may dominate interactions with friends and acquaintances. Misery likes company for sure it seems.

Physical pain is part of being human. It's a signal that something is amiss. In the same way that a smoke alarm's beeping gives warning of household fire, pain serves as an internal feedback loop to give a message. Only people with the rare disorder of allodynia cannot feel pain. Generally, they have very short lives because their essential warning mechanisms are absent.

Physical pathways of pain can be adequately treated with present-day pain management approaches. These may include specific forms of exercise, dietary changes to increase cell nourishment and decrease weight, prescription and over-the-counter medications, and even special formulas and administration routes developed by compounding pharmacies.[1] In addition, a large array of complementary modalities is available to offer holistic, integrative approaches such as the energy-oriented interventions given in this volume. Current medical standards have established adequate pain management as a patient health-care right in most states, and many states require health-care professionals to take one-day pain management courses as part of the license renewal process.

How We "Shrink" Our Lives

Like most readers, I can personally attest to the difficulty of centering, meditating, or holding a positive outlook when pain predominates. I recall the ways hip pain led me to explore numerous complementary modalities such as acupuncture, energy healing, chiropractic, somatic therapies, and depth psychotherapy. I learned much and still employ the many insights I gained from these modalities. Denial of the significance of pain kept me limping until my whole outlook on life became increasingly constricted.

In the eighth year of bone and back pain, I wanted to try a more traditional route and chose to get an X ray. The physician was amazed that anyone was able to walk with such a degenerated hip. What I have learned since the replacement surgery has taught me not to put things off until my life becomes difficult. When other methods no longer help and activities start to shrink, it's wise to seek specific medical assistance.

Nevertheless, I affirm the value of exploring complementary/alternative approaches first as a useful way to learn about oneself and the ways mind, body, and spirit are constantly interacting. More invasive chemical or surgical interventions are available as a last resort. Unless there is a need for acute care and immediate action, such complementary approaches as acupuncture, acupressure, Qigong, yoga, and energy-oriented therapies are a good first line of defense.

Ongoing, chronic pain can "shrink" one's life. Activities become constricted, emotions fray, sleep is interrupted, and insomnia curtails opportunity for restorative sleep. An estimated "fifty million Americans live with chronic pain today; it is the number one cause of adult disability."[2] More than half the health-care professionals who attend my workshops suffer from various chronic pain conditions. Unfortunately, these glum figures are accompanied by beliefs that chronic pain cannot be changed and "one has to learn to live with it." Such limiting beliefs especially apply to the elderly who are often underdiagnosed and undertreated.

A hopeful message tells us, "When pain is treated effectively, the person's quality of life increases and negative outcomes decrease."[3] Multimodal approaches that integrate adequate medication with complementary interventions, such as activating the body's energy system, seem to work best. A dynamic formula for using the body's natural resources and self-hypnosis to resolve chronic pain is written by colleague Maggie Phillips.[4] She emphasizes energizing ourselves rather than catastrophizing about pain, and healing not only the body but also our emotional and spiritual dimensions. Energy therapies can provide a powerful adjunct to managing and even ameliorating pain distress.

Suffering Is Optional

Suffering is qualitatively different from physical pain. Physiological pain mechanisms have been well studied and involve a number of bodily pathways: The signal or pain stimulus initiates at a certain location in the body, it travels via neurotransmitters cell-to-cell along the dorsal afferent fibers to the dorsal horn of the spinal column, and finally reaches the brain to impact the pain-sensing centers. The mind can then interpret the message and engage in a number of choices. It can:

• Feel the pain.

• Block all or part of the pain.

- Exaggerate the pain.

- Feel the pain and forget it because something else takes precedence.

- Distort the pain sensation.

- Interpret the pain signal.

- Focus on the pain and attach strong emotions to it.

According to Buddhist philosophy, suffering relates to the emotional distress of worry and anxiety generated within an individual. Fear of more pain, not the pain itself, exacerbates suffering. The distress known as suffering can be triggered by physical pain, but it can also be about any thought that comes to mind.

Examples cited earlier spoke of the distress experienced in everyday life issues ranging from impediments to living such as flat tires or balky cell phones to serious family conflicts and alienation by loved ones. Suffering occurs when we attempt to interpret events not caused by our actions. We may ask, "Why does this always happen to me?" or attack ourselves, as in "What is the matter with me?" and conclude, "No one appreciates me. I'm losing my touch. I'm not useful any more."

A direct path to suffering is made by attaching catastrophic meaning to a minor glitch. People of any age can forget names, book titles, or peripheral events, yet interpreting simple forgetting to mean your mind is failing and/or you're losing it permanently is common among older people. This creates untold suffering. Perhaps it is good to forget some things, especially trivia, when we've accumulated so much knowledge from living over half a century. It would be detrimental to recall every detail we ever heard!

The mind responds to unconscious commands. If we want to retire by abdicating from lifelong learning or participation in the community, the mind finds situations requiring stepping back and being passive. If we want to be miserable, there will always be opportunity for fear-generated suffering. Negative thinking creates direct results not only in the form of limiting beliefs, but also in the form of limited gene expression and reduction of health-promoting messaging from the DNA. Similarly, negative reflections about physical pain serve to increase pain's disabling effects.

As we come to distinguish the difference between physical pain and the psychological factors involved in suffering, we recognize how closely they are interrelated. Both need to be addressed to diminish distress. Remarkably, both emotional suffering and physical pain respond well to energetic interventions by inviting changes in perception and hope of relief.

Numerous research studies demonstrate relief of physical and emotional pain with energy modalities such as TT, HT, Reiki, energy medicine, and energy psychology.[5] Some of the possible mechanisms for this effect include: 1) increased production of endorphins, the body's natural pain-relieving chemical messengers; 2) encouragement and support of gene expression; 3) distraction of the mind in a possible placebo effect; 4) release of blockages to balanced energy flows; and 5) movement toward a "tipping point" because there's momentum toward greater comfort and positive emotion.

Tim's Story: Willingness to Go Beyond the Diagnosis

Tim had been diagnosed with the life-threatening immune system disorder of lupus. From that day on, Tim interpreted every small ache or distress to mean that his body's cells were being destroyed by the disease. All he could see was a future of degeneration, dependence on others, and death. The power of a serious diagnosis without additional information can serve as a *nocebo*, with negative implications, instead of its opposite, a *placebo*, a powerful mental suggestion for relief and well-being. Tim's family insisted on second opinions, more information, and complementary approaches for self-care. Grumbling and wincing, Tim agreed to their wishes and found, to his surprise, a wealth of resources to stave off dependency and helplessness. Of course, it took time, unending encouragement from family members, and Tim's willingness to participate in the expanded program. Years later, he is still active and talks to his diagnosis of lupus by joking "Ha! You thought you owned me, but I didn't let you!"

It's always best to have pain medically evaluated and receive as much information as possible. The following exercises encourage you to learn from your pain sensations and find ways of diminishing pain reliably. The exercises utilize your energy system—the breath, the meridian network via its acupoints, and the charkas, the body's "energy stations." The exercises also seem to increase the efficacy of medication, so you may over time notice a diminished need for any medications you are taking.

Exercise 13.1 More Life via Your Helping Intention

1. Allow yourself to sit or lie comfortably with the breath gently expanding the diaphragm as you inhale. Make sure the exhalation is long and slow.

2. Breathe softness and warmth into the painful area. Send your caring intention to the hurting portion of the body.

3. Make a tight fist and release it slowly to a long count of ten, feeling each muscle group in your hand relax slowly.

4. Repeat several more times while continuing to send loving thoughts to the identified part of the body. Soften the colors around it.

5. Notice any differences in how you feel.

Exercise 13.2 Healing Affirmations Embedded in the Body

1. While gently rubbing or holding the tender spot on the left side of the upper chest, state out loud, "Even though I have this pain, I deeply and completely love and accept myself."

2. If the last part of the affirmation is troublesome for you, you can use other phrases such as, "I'm learning to accept myself" or simply "I deserve to feel better."

3. The first part of the affirmation can also be used to address underlying fears with, "Even though I fear I might never be free of this pain, I still choose to _____ (complete with your chosen statement)."

4. Repeat your selected phrase several times until it feels comfortable and you can easily remember it. Write it down, or make up a song or poem about it.

Exercise 13.3 Releasing Fear and Installing Positive Thoughts via the Acupoints

1. Starting at the place where the eyebrow meets the nose, tap or touch, alternating sides, while stating, "I now choose to release my fear of more pain. This is not all of me" (or use words with similar intent).

2. Continue tapping through the acupoint sequence given in figure 3.5. Tap each acupoint ten to fifteen times.

3. Complete by tapping or holding each point starting at step 1 while stating your positive goal, as in "Many forms of help, including medication and this work, are available to me."

4. Note how you feel when you think of available help.

Exercise 13.4 Releasing Fear and Installing Positive Thoughts via the Chakras

1. Starting at the crown, touch or spin with the hands in a counter-clockwise fashion while stating, "I now release fear of more pain. It is not all of me."

2. Continue downward through the seven major chakras as shown in figure 3.3 and end with an exultation.

3. Complete by moving upward from the base with a clockwise spin over each center while stating your positive goal, "I now attract the resources I need to manage this pain. Love and support surround me. I am doing my best to heal."

4. Note how verbalizing your positive goal makes you feel.

Exercise 13.5 Tapping the Thyroid Meridian for Relief

Another tool for relief can be found by tapping on the thyroid meridian acupoint, which appears to generalize healing intention to all parts of the body.[6]

1. While sitting or lying down comfortably, gently touch the painful area and set your positive intention with a statement such as "Relief is on its way."

2. Use one hand to tap on the acupoint between the last two knuckles of the other hand (on the thyroid meridian, also known as the triple warmer or tri-heater meridian).

3. Tap gently on this acupoint thirty to fifty times while affirming your wish to feel better and sending kindness to the selected area. Breathe deeply and fully.

4. Note how you feel afterward.

Exercise 13.6 Moving Healing Hands over a Painful Area

In the Healing Touch practices, clear intention through centering practices can be used to energize your hands for self-care and relief.[7]

1. With the breath allow yourself to bring in the unlimited energy flow from the beauty of nature.

2. Let the warmth of this breath flow from your heart center to your hands to increase their vitality. You may also squeeze or rub the hands together to energize them. Continue until the hands feel warm and vibrant.

3. Bring the hands near the painful area of your body and gently sweep from above the area downward several times while continuing to keep the breath smooth, strong, and steady.

4. Repeat several times during the day and notice any changes such as a lighter sensation in the area.

Using Healing Touch gently sweep a painful area of the body.

Each of the exercises are can be modified to fit your needs. They return to you the power to help your body. Some studies also propose increased efficacy of pain medication with these maneuvers. You may find the exercises a helpful addition to any medication you are using. Recalling how intention affects the body's messaging signals, the use of subtle energies appears to activate remembered wellness in body, mind, and spirit.

Freda's Story: Better Than Winning a Lawsuit for Pain

It's especially difficult to address pain management issues with people who are unassertive, poor, and elderly. Freda had all three of these issues. As the sole caregiver for a profoundly retarded twenty-four-year-old son, she was also raising a healthy sixteen-year-old daughter. When I met her on referral from her social worker, Freda was awash in pain and suffered from insomnia. After a severe car accident caused by a careless driver six months earlier, Freda was overwhelmed by all aspects of her life. A lawsuit was pending to pay for some of her medical expenses. Because she was not yet old enough for Medicare, she exhausted her meager financial resources in attempts to get medical help for intractable neck and back pain. Freda's physician prescribed medication that did not touch the pain and only made her sleepy. Finally, the doctor prescribed a cane for a misdiagnosis of "arthritis."

My first steps in helping Freda were to establish simple things she could do, such as establishing adequate pain management with over-the-counter pills. With a regular schedule of medication, Freda had some respite from pain while saving her high-potency and expensive prescriptions for nighttime sleep. We gradually added a high-protein diet and moderate exercise. More important for Freda was learning to be effectively assertive in communicating with both her doctor and attorney, neither of whom showed much interest in her case. Eventually, she was strong enough to fire them both and find a nurse practitioner who could prescribe an effective pain management regimen. After Freda learned how to interview for better and low-cost legal aid, she retained an attorney who was sympathetic to her cause.

With these two professionals well in place, I taught Freda the pain management techniques detailed here. She took to them immediately. "I can do something to help myself!" she exclaimed. It was as if a treasure box had been opened for her. There was still pain, but her endless suffering ceased.

Freda received an MRI after a long year of haggling with insurance companies. It showed three cracked neck vertebrae, which were not visible on the initial X rays. Knowing the cause of pain generated some comfort.

The lawsuit against the careless motorist went awry because he was uninsured at the time of the accident. The misdiagnosis of arthritis also worked against Freda. Pain perception is so subjective that many insurance companies and their hired physicians can reinterpret patients' testimonies. Freda finally received a minimal settlement. However, she proudly told me, "That's only money, but what you gave me back was my ability to help myself. It was far better than winning a lawsuit for pain!"

Soothing Self-Care Travels Faster

James Dillard's fascinating book, *The Chronic Pain Solution*, cites studies showing how soothing techniques actually travel faster than pain along the neural pathways. This suggests mechanisms for decreasing or even blocking pain perception. For example, an itch or pain sensation travels at about 0.5 to 5 millimeters per second along the neurons. Massage and light touch travel approximately 15 to 25 millimeters per second, whereas the body's electromagnetic signals with which energy therapies work travel at much faster speeds of 35 to 75 millimeters per second.[8]

These studies help to understand why massage and touch are so necessary in healing. They also explain how energy approaches work most quickly to reach the brain's interpretive centers and provide relaxation and relief from anxiety and discomfort.

Often, in working with multimodal pain management, it is a matter of which signal gets to the brain first. In the case of severe pain, it would be prudent to take medication to give basic relief and then add the energy modalities. The guidance of competent medical care is, of course, always needed when using new techniques or attempting to change established pain management protocols.

＊＊＊＊

To summarize, the energy approaches suggested here for pain relief are easy to learn, highly portable, and can be combined with other therapies. The latter may include somatic therapies such as massage and bodywork, counseling, physical therapy, and medication protocols. Energy therapies further relieve the negative emotional reactions related to pain; these reactions include anxiety, panic, and fear. Thoughts and beliefs blocking healing efforts can also be modified or revised. Quality of life can best exist when we address the deeper causes of internal emotional suffering.

Chapter Fourteen
Fully Conscious Endings

A radical demand on us is the discovery and acceptance of our lives as a series of movements or passages. . .we are always passing from one phase to the next, gaining and losing someone, some place, some thing.
—Henri J. M. Nouwen

We acknowledge the reality of movements or passages as we let the words of this chapter's opening quote sink in. Life has a beginning, a middle, and an end. The key to a successful second half of life lies in effectively facing change and loss. We have no choice about our birth, but paths in adulthood lie open. Given the second chances offered from midlife onward, we can actualize our life's dream in meaningful ways. We can contemplate how we wish our relationships to be, what we still want to create, and, certainly, how we want to depart. In the long run, how we heal our life at any given moment is much more important than our dying.

Experiencing change in a conscious way is like having practice sessions. For example, moving from one neighborhood to another can be welcomed as meeting a new community or it can be interpreted as a loss of the known. We can honor feelings of sadness, acknowledge friendships, however brief or casual, and consciously say our good-byes. Or we can ignore the feelings and make unrealistic promises for the future. Despite assurances to the contrary, relationships are seldom the same after a physical move. Only the most active friendships can overcome geographic barriers, and even e-mails peter out after a while.

Conscious preparation for dying can begin with acknowledging "little deaths." "These little deaths include changes, losses, and disappointments at work or with family and friends; goals not accomplished; or temporary illnesses.... These little deaths also can occur as realizations that we should release old behaviors and relationships that no longer serve us in order to allow room for new behaviors, relationships and possibilities."[1]

Life is about change. From an energetic perspective, physical death is only a passage, a transition into another form of consciousness. The wisest teachers of our time believe consciousness continues in some other form beyond the cessation of physical life. Those new paths can best be captured metaphorically or symbolically. One image, for instance, proposes that we die into awakening, from the dream known as consensus reality into a much larger, more spacious reality. Possibly, poetry best captures the flavor of ongoing, expanded consciousness after the body gives out:

Like a raindrop falling

A dewdrop glistening delight

We are part of water

Returning to the rivers of our birth

The wide oceans of space...

Like a beam of light

Leaving heaven's sun

We nourish earth's life,

And take up many forms.

Then the luminous spark

Returns safely to its source

Our energetic home...

A Ghastly Scenario

Bestselling author Larry Dossey, MD, reminds us that consciousness is nonlocal, unlimited by space and time. There is an innately nonlocal part of us that cannot die. In his eyes, the idea of coming into a human life devoid of meaning and being gone when physical life ceases creates a "ghastly scenario."[2]

Belief in consciousness tied only to the existence of the body quite naturally fosters fears of death. The idea of being bound only to the physical body supports the short-term thinking, materialism, and consumerism so prevalent in our culture. It supports a medical culture for extending life at all costs, even when quality of life is diminished or absent, or accompanied by irreversible physical changes. Many medical practitioners view death as failure on their part. The human soul, one's life essence, loses its dignity when interventions to sustain the body exceed the quality of life. Given the present medical scenario, the soul may be dying in anguish long before the physical body gives out.

Dying well and moving into a new existence is an act of faith, a confidence in something beyond our present knowing. It requires choices, trust in the unknown, and willingness to release attachments.

Lucy's Story: Belief in Lights Out

Lucy shared feelings of profound loss when her business partner of thirty years died suddenly. The friend, beset with several illnesses, died while sitting in front of her television set and was not discovered for five days. One point of view might celebrate her tranquil exit from discomfort into her next stage of life. Another view might focus on the humor of a departure in such a mundane setting and hoping the last program she saw was somehow inspiring to her. Lucy, however, became absorbed with the horror of what the neighbors might have discovered on finding the body and the sheer loneliness of her friend's death. She believed, "When you're gone, there's only blackness—that's it."

After mulling things over a while, Lucy decided to offer comfort to the surviving family. To bring a sense of closure and to comfort herself, she recalled the many intimate times shared in the years of collaboration. What seemed to be left after those activities was a disturbing sense of emptiness and loss. However it occurs, the actual moment of death is brief. It pales in comparison to decades of shared adventures the friends had. Allowing a sense of her friend's ongoing presence or energy in another form would have given Lucy a much richer, more comforting grief experience.

Many people, including present company, find the idea of ongoing consciousness in some form much more palatable and more hopeful than just darkness—lights out. The mystery of what lies beyond the veil seems unknowable except for the reports from those who have been there. Nearly five million people have experienced a near-death phenomenon. They largely report pleasant, beautiful surroundings, meetings with loved ones, and reluctance to return to this side of life.[3] It's hard to deny the experiences of these "space travelers."

Numerous caregivers also report shifts in and out of different levels of consciousness in patients close to transition. Such "visits" to what lies beyond present-day life are almost always associated with pleasure, freedom, and a sense of connecting with loved ones and one's home. When the founder of the American Holistic Nurses Association, Charly McGuire, was close to death recently, her powerful consciousness connected with deep peace and beauty on the other side. All caregivers were inspired by her presence even though she was no longer able to speak. Her actual transition was a graceful slipping into another form of being.

After-death encounters support ongoing human consciousness as well. One study reports a variety of brief but powerful positive encounters with someone deceased in the form of visions, dreams, lost-things-found, symbolic messages, and a strong sense of the person's presence.[4]

The reality of physical life's ending spurs us on to find our life's meaning and purpose, and to develop spiritual resources. If we really had forever to live, we might never feel the imperative to actualize our life's dream!

Comforting "Little Deaths"

The profession of nursing has been most intensively involved in care of the seriously ill and dying. A great blossoming of publications has come forth in recent years from nursing educators, healing practitioners, and theorists.

One poignant study reports the lived experience of people with serious debilitating illnesses.[5] When there is major loss of physical capabilities, connectedness to others also often diminishes, resulting in social isolation. Numerous issues were reported by all participants in the study: the reality of confronting and facing loss, dealing with fluctuating emotions, making needed lifestyle changes, and gaining control of an altered life direction. Fear of pain, losing control, and becoming dependent consistently superseded fears of dying. The helplessness of a debilitating illness challenges caregivers and patients alike to find ways of breaking through isolation to communicate needs, maintaining supportive relationships, keeping as much independence as possible, and making peace with one's new situation.

Although it may be difficult to believe something good can come from life-threatening illness, finding helpful learning is an empowering choice. Serving as a role model for family and friends spurs many ill people to value the uniqueness of their experience and find creativity in overcoming obstacles. Writers may turn their challenges into a new book or journal article. Other people who face obstacles of long-term illness note their increased sensitivity to others. Being curtailed in motion can lead to more interest in music, the arts, poetry, and Internet chat rooms. A major gift for some in times of enforced quiet is feeling the power of love and connection with others and the increased commitment to live fully in the present, one moment at a time.

One of my painting friends had a severe car accident that rendered her paraplegic. Her paintings produced in the ten years after the accident have won many awards and are regarded as local treasures. She tells me the quiet of sitting has helped her to shape her pictures long before she actually commits an idea to canvas.

Pioneers in nursing, and now the counseling professions as well, have been exploring energetic ways to calm the emotional roller coaster associated with profound changes in health. It's comforting to know that self-care and pain-soothing exercises can quickly activate feel-good messages and enhance the effectiveness of medication. It's also consoling to know of numerous health-care professionals who are engaged in palliative care, which includes a variety of energy therapies and permits that bypass the constraints of hospice regulations.[6]

Healing Touch and Therapeutic Touch practitioners actively involved in end-of-life care now report a number of significant outcomes. One study shows a significant decrease in physical symptoms, less change in overall functioning, and no change in interpersonal relationships when HT and/or TT were employed. There was worsening in all three areas in the control groups who did not receive energetic interventions. The researcher reported, "Responses from those in the HT group included increased relaxation, increased relief of pain, spiritual benefit, increased calmness, and improved breathing."[7]

Gary's Story: Covering all the Bases

As a Healing Touch practitioner and energy psychologist, I have worked with a number of clients with severe illness. Gary, a physicist, was an especially challenging client, as nothing was believable to him unless it had literal, scientific proof. Nevertheless, facing a life-threatening illness in the form of a brain tumor led him to question his life's meaning and purpose. He did not want any fluff or metaphysics. I told him about near-death experiences of people who clinically died and were brought back to life. This made him quite thoughtful, as he wanted proof of something beyond physical life.

Throughout my time with Gary, I taught him some of the energy interventions given in this book while also allowing him to vent his concerns and fears. His biggest stumbling block to leaving peacefully turned out to be his apathetic, estranged relationship with his daughters. He learned to practice the hope meditation (exercise 12.1) and the forgiveness exercise (14.1) and then sent each of the daughters letters inviting them to meet with him. In his own way, Gary began to heal distortions in his life. He came to recognize the gift of the illness in giving him a second chance to mend his relationships.

After family peace was restored, Gary's illness went into remission. I did not see him for several years. Gary sent me a letter stating much had actually improved including his physical health. Although he never agreed with my mystical leanings toward ongoing consciousness in the next stages of life, he ended the letter by saying, "I've decided you get what you wish for in the time after death. I know what I want so I better ask for it. I would like a beautiful meadow with music and lots of dancing with my friends."

Ask for What You Want

Each of us is in charge of our own living and dying. The two are continuously intertwined: While living, we are actually on our way to dying; while dying, we have the opportunity to live most fully. Living in fear may actually create daily psychological deaths. Choosing what you want for your death can become a meditation on behalf of your life.

Gandhi was one of the most remarkable men of the twentieth century. He came from humble beginnings and took on the British empire in seeking freedom for India. When asked how he dealt with daily threats on his life, his paraphrased reply was, "I only die once.

Those who fear death die hundreds of times." His confidence and focused energy led the poor and oppressed to major victories over imperial forces. When an assassin pulled out his gun in close proximity, Gandhi is reported to have said "Om," a blessing of peace, before the bullet reached him. It was only a moment, but his whole life was filled with blessings for his nation.

Paula Gaa Stover is a remarkable holistic nurse I've known for more than twenty years. When she was diagnosed with cancer at age fifty-three, she faced bilateral mastectomy along with other surgical and chemical interventions. She saw it as an opportunity to make a 180-degree turn toward conscious living, fighting off disease with love for herself, her family, and her friends. In her article "Surviving to Share," she writes of her conscious choices while in the hands of the medical environment.[8] First, she assembled nine reliable friends who agreed to take turns at her bedside giving unconditional love to her. They also agreed to make no demands on her. She posted a message on her door for every doctor, nurse, and caregiver who entered, which stated, "While in this room, please celebrate my good fortune in finding this cancer early. Your positive emotional tone will help me set a healing path of strength and vitality. This life event is just another adventure, one that challenges and motivates me to live even more fully. Please know this: There is nothing to fear. God is completely in charge here. Thanks so much for all you are doing to assist in my recovery."

Asking for what she wanted from her friends and caregivers gave Paula an appropriate sense of power over her own life. Many people I work with become emotion-bound and ineffective when facing their own physical ailments or attempting to help friends in need. Asking someone or yourself what kind of help is really wanted is a great gift. The answer is often something very simple: "Just be with me," "Just listen," "Play some music," "Laugh with me," or "Let's remember good times."

From an energetic point of view, we learn to practice the gift of full presence. You need to ask yourself: What is really important? And what do I really want? Physicians and caregivers do not read your mind. You are the captain of your healing team. Don't let anyone talk you into a treatment in which you do not believe. Ask lots of questions of your caregivers. The more proactive you are, the more likely you are to get what you wish.

Exploring the Mystery

Plato's observation that no one believes they will die might be viewed as humankind's intuitive perception about the immortality of consciousness. Having explored ourselves as energetic beings with multidimensional layers and vibrational pathways, we see the physical body as only a part of who we really are. From an energetic perspective, we can view the physical body as a temporary container for our consciousness, just as scientists acknowledge the localized brain as only the temporary casing for the larger nonlocal mind. Consciousness not only resides in our cells and DNA, it persists in the form of vibrations that allow us to access intuitive knowing, to sense others' love over distances, and to sense the presence of those who have moved beyond physical life.

Human denial about the reality of life's end is pervasive and may help to fuel the media's obsession with youth. Until Elisabeth Kübler-Ross, MD, began teaching and writing in the 1970s about death as the final stage of growth,[9] the topic was taboo even in hospital settings. It is still rare for a public figure to admit having a terminal illness or discuss the possibility of dying, and even rarer for the public to accept such a reality. In spite of giving much vital energy to public service in raising awareness about spinal cord injuries, when actor Christopher Reeves died after ten years of dealing with his devastating injury, his passing was met with seeming shock by the media and questions of "foul play." There was marked inability to accept what may well have been his well-deserved time to move on.

Another form of denial is avoiding the topic of death entirely while one is healthy. There seems to be a subconscious belief that if one does not speak about death, it will not happen. Only when the body signals that it is wearing out and physical care is mandated do most people actually face the possibility of leaving their earthly home. Avoiding this topic does not prevent it from occurring, however. Our chances of experiencing physical death are 100 percent, as best as we know, so we might as well talk about it.

We all carry a terminal diagnosis. The physical body eventually wears out. Anyone can die in any decade; it's just a bit more likely to happen in the later decades of life.

We have many choices for moving into this challenging domain. Just as we awaken from sleep dreams to a new day, it's entirely possible we'll awaken from the physical body to a finer, higher vibrational energy. With great courage, one of my clients with a life-threatening illness recently affirmed, "Until I actually pass on, I plan to go on living fully to the best of my abilities."

Energy Self-Help to the Rescue!

Since physical death is seen as failure in the current allopathic medical model, lack of discussion deprives most of us of opportunities to explore pathways to understanding our transitions from life. Energy-based approaches have much to offer even when full relief of physical symptoms is not possible in the case of chronic pain or long-term illness. For those whose distress is primarily emotional, energy approaches offer ways of supporting inner wellness. For those with physical distress or pain, energetic approaches such as centering, working with affirmations, and tapping acupoints bring a rich variety of resources for empowerment.

These are powerful changes, which go beyond usual experiences of therapy. We can move beyond symptom relief to higher levels of well-being. Even better, energetic approaches seem to access creative potentials by demonstrating other ways of viewing death and dying.

Jack's Story: A Life Well Completed

Jack was dying of metastatic lung cancer at the beginning of his sixty-fourth year. The devastating diagnosis brought him to doctors who predicted his death within a few months even after aggressive chemotherapy. With the help of his daughter Terri, Jack was able to express his fears of losing control and the dying process. Terri, supported by her energy-oriented therapist, helped him to see there were many aspects of his life where he could actively take control and facilitate healing.

Jack had complex family relationships. Due to his history of alcoholism and inflicting physical abuse, Jack was both loved and hated by his children. In the last months of his life, he had an unprecedented opportunity to make amends with each of them and to seek their forgiveness wherever possible.

Jack actively worked to better himself and his family relationships while he was physically dying. He was amazed at how each family member responded to his outreach in different but positive ways. He used centering, heart chakra balancing, and affirmations to help him deal with the wide spectrum of feelings. Through this work, he also developed a strong sense of personal faith. Despite declining physical health, Jack became actively involved in healing his emotional fears, family relationships, and spiritual connection to Higher Power. On the final day of his life, he was surrounded by his children and relatives—finally living his life dream of being part of a loving family. All present stated how their lives had become enriched because of Jack's unrelenting efforts to actively seek forgiveness.

Long after the memorial services, Jack's family continued to discuss how they were healed, helped, and made whole by his courageous efforts in the last days of life. Terri continued to feel her father's presence, especially when completing graduate studies. She sensed his energy supporting her as she struggled with academic details. Although his physical body was no longer present, Terri could feel her father's humor, caring, and encouraging words. She speculated, "I wonder if maybe...maybe some portion of a person's energy field continues to be present with loved ones after biological death. I certainly feel Dad's presence by my shoulder every day. It's so precious!"

Exercise 14.1 Heart Center Balancing

People of all ages struggle with what to do when they receive a devastating diagnosis or when medical practitioners state they have nothing further to offer. The adventuresome ones start by acknowledging their grief and nurturing the heart center. This exercise can help you do this.

1. Relaxing fully with several exhalations, connect with the reality of your situation.

2. Affirm with gentle rubbing on the tender spot on the left side of the upper chest, "Even though I have been told_____(fill in the specifics), _____I deeply and profoundly honor and respect myself. I trust my pathway to healing in whatever dimension is possible."

3. Comfort the grieving heart center by gently moving both hands clockwise over the mid-chest heart chakra.

4. Find words that speak to your innermost soul. Examples: "I love you," "I will listen to you," "We'll make this journey together," "I trust in the Unknowable," and "I rejoice in beauty around me."

5. Make a list of what you still would like to do, especially noting anything incomplete in your relationships with others. Appreciate

your creativity in handling the new situation, in reinventing your-self in light of your new reality.

Exercise 14.2 Forgiveness Is Free!

Holding grudges and resentments generates a heavy burden on the human soul. Forgiveness of oneself and others is free; it does not cost anything except letting go of a bit of ego pride. It is also quite easy if we so choose; all that is required is our willingness and a path-way such as this one.

1. After doing the heart center balancing exercise (see previous), think of the times and places in your life you held a grudge toward someone.

2. While moving both hands over your heart center, visualize each person, alive or deceased, one at a time, in front of you. State as honestly as you can, "I forgive you for_____(state specifics)."

3. If this is difficult for you, start at the crown chakra and work downward through each chakra (see figure 3.3), spinning the hands counterclockwise while releasing the resentment. Affirm you deserve to be free of this burden. Give an exultation when you have done so.

4. Alternately, start at the eyebrow acupoint and tap to release and forgive, using a statement such as "I now release my resentment toward _____ for _____." Work with the other acupoints (see figure 3.5) in a similar fashion.

5. Note how this can be freeing and uplifting. Remind yourself often that no one obligates you to hold a resentment. It's only a choice and you have decided it's no longer the right choice for you.

Exercise 14.3 The Inner Smile

This exercise came to me many years ago from a Buddhist friend. It reminds me of the simple wisdom of the Dalai Lama.

1. After making yourself comfortable, think of something occurring recently that made you smile.

2. Take the quality of the inner smile to your head and let it surround your midbrain (the limbic center of the emotional brain and the pituitary and pineal glands) like a warm light or a soft touch. Feel the smile there with kindly appreciation.

3. Take the inner smile to the throat area and the thyroid gland; surround it with a sense of warmth or a color.

4. Take the inner smile to the heart, the lungs, each of the internal organs—liver, spleen, pancreas, kidneys, and bladder, the digestive system, sexual organs and genitals, and the major joints.

5. Let the whole body resonate with the kindly reflections of the inner smile. Gently let yourself come back to full awareness.

Exercise 14.4 Practicing the Art of Presence

Approaching someone who is ill or dying brings us face-to-face with our own being. We ask: What can I give? Or if you are the patient, others may ask: What do you need?

Usually, the list of someone seriously ill or in transition is short: "Let things flow," "Just be with me," "Let me know how I made a difference to you," or "Stay with me awhile."

1. Becoming present to yourself and another person begins with centering. Always start with balancing yourself (see exercise 4.1).

2. Let your heart center open by gently holding your hands over your heart.

3. Acknowledge the gift of the present moment. No past or future, just now.

4. Note the energy of the room when you are fully present to yourself and the other person.

5. This is one of the times when we come closest to collapsing the wave of ordinary time-space. Appreciate the gift of the other person. Accept the gift of who you are.

6. Make sure you are fully alert before departing, especially if you are taking on more linear tasks such as driving.

****

It appears the physical body is meant to be left behind while our spiritual being expands in consciousness. We can make choices to support well-being and ask for what is needed. We can dance into our aliveness while we are on our way to the unknown next stage of life.

Chapter Fifteen
Keep Evolving!

We must always change, renew, rejuvenate ourselves;
otherwise we harden.
—Johann Wolfgang v. Goethe

No Longer Content to Sleepwalk through Life

To summarize this exploration, let's look at the expanded identity for us as awake, empowered elders. No longer willing to sleepwalk as helpless victims of time, we are now the intrepid heroes who have survived journeys through life's physical and emotional challenges. Steps to facilitate ongoing evolution include establishing energetic balance rapidly, releasing dysfunctional beliefs, seeking increased flexibility, and applying energy resources to daily issues. We may also seek to bring life-enhancing, transpersonal awareness into every moment. With these strengths in place, we access inner wisdom, intuition, hope, and new perspectives. We refresh ourselves by connecting with nature's unlimited gifts of vitality and inventiveness. We are also learning how to nurture ourselves so we can deal with pain and choose what's right for our living—and our dying.

Instead of merely surviving life's traumas and losses, we can move through adversity with the support of *qi* resources given in this book. In place of mere survival and getting by, we now substitute active, joyous "thrival."

Stretching into Possibilities

For many, the idea of thriving may mean rewriting worn-out tales about aging. Cultural myths are the framework for beliefs generated to explain the past, understand the present, and direct the future. The idea of thriving in mature decades may require radical new contexts. The stories about aging that we tell ourselves must include the vision of full-energy living until our final, courageous moments.

Joseph Campbell was the leading authority on cultural myths made famous by a series of television interviews with Bill Moyers toward the end of his life.[1] Campbell recalls the myth of the hero's journey repeated in many forms throughout human history. The young person sets out to conquer the world and ends up wounded and challenged. Bloodied and bowed, older and wiser, he returns to his home to bring wisdom to his people and to empower them. In British mythology, this wise elder becomes the Grail King, guardian of the highest spiritual potentialities of human consciousness. The myth of the hero's journey and the mission of the Grail King give an inspiring vision of the future for elders.

We may also need to revise personal myths about creativity, as they may be too limited to encompass full thriving. Innovators are often depicted as unusual people with special gifts, who have artistic, moody temperaments and behave in erratic ways. This pervasive myth can serve as an excuse for not taking risks or ignoring the imagination. The new definition of creativity now includes all intelligent people who want to develop their potentials and live as fully as possible. We are on a quest for a purposeful life filled with self-esteem and vitality. We enlightened elders are the artists of our lives.

Understandably, there are risks whenever we try something new. Exploring new behaviors or acting in a different ways takes effort. Like the sailor who is continually correcting his course with changes in wind and currents, we need to adjust our direction as we evolve. When we accept innate creativity as our human birthright, we learn that we are much more capable than ever imagined. Later life becomes an unfolding, exciting adventure.

One way of exploring the vast possibilities awaiting us is via the metaphor of chaos theory, frequently called systems theory. This recent theory has a humility that is lacking in the hubris of the linear, cause-and-effect thinking of Newtonian physics. Systems theory presumes the high probability that all systems will go into turbulence, or disorder. It also suggests such perturbations will lead to the emergence of order at another level of integration, even when, from our limited viewpoints, we cannot see the ongoing complexities and subtle transformations. The relevance of these metaphors to life artistry lies in their implications for tolerating ambiguity and embodying open-ended thinking. "Chaos [theory], it turns out, is as much about what we *can't* know as it is about certainty....It's about letting go, accepting limits, and celebrating magic and mystery."[2]

As we explore the underlying interconnections in our lives, we become more attuned to subtle movements, hidden patterns, and unpredictable nuances. The life artist is the person who is willing to embrace life's uncertainties. Although this may temporarily feel like loss of control, it embraces tolerance for ambiguity. Whereas the fanatic attempts to cover uncertainties with lists, structures, and guarantees, the creative person faces the unknown by paying attention to irregular orders present in nonlinear systems such as the weather. The life artist trusts that a new path, a new synthesis, can emerge from apparent turbulence.

This does not mean being "spacey" or ungrounded. As we link with our energy resources, we find the steady center of our strengths. The resources for energy balance are as close as the next conscious breath or a specific energy exercise. The fires of age can glow steadily and be rekindled instantly whenever we choose to use these resources.

The new story of awakened thriving permits an ongoing saga filled with curiosity, creative exploration, and positive expectancy.

This is especially true when taking the inevitable journey from physical life into unknown realms beyond.

Maps for the Journey

More people are now entering and staying in the second half of life than at any previous time in history. Most have little preparation for meeting the challenges and opportunities of their additional thirty to fifty years. A map is needed to build muscle to make the most out of the bonus years and become eloquent transformative agents.

Two choices you can make have been shown to transform mere longevity into high-quality, healthful living. One is building loving relationships and the other is deepening your spirituality. Cardiologist Dean Ornish concludes that love, intimacy, and relatedness are better predictors of health after heart disease than all other factors including medicines, diet, exercise, and stress management.[3] Studies show spiritual involvement adds seven years, on average, to one's life while also expanding confidence and trust in forces greater than oneself.[4]

Another rewarding map lies in the work of my friend and collaborator on many projects, David Gruder. He describes seven wise passions for anyone who wishes to move into maturity and seasoned integrity. The first four passions address necessary personal work that comes from being teachable, committing to self-care, being able to discern truth from spin, and harvesting the learning from challenges. The socially oriented passions that also need to be expressed are the right use of power, ability to work synergistically with others, and acceptance of generational responsibility by becoming a steward of our planet.[5]

Here are some other guideposts. Allow yourself to resonate with each one of them and note which ones call out to you for further development:

- Drop the idea of retirement. Choose instead to reinvent yourself every few years. Pace yourself for the long run.

- Accept where you currently are in relation to your physical and emotional health and engage in creative problem solving. Connect with others, and think how you could help another person with similar issues.

- Deal with emotions engendered by disappointments.

- Love more, expect less.

- Move through fear and thoughts of defeat.

- Recognize fear as a constriction of your entire being. Treat yourself for any fears as they arises. FEAR (acronym for false evidence appearing real) restricts healthy gene expression and creates the opposite of loving, learning, and thriving.

- Affirm your strengths, talents, and gifts.

- Eschew boredom.

- Do something you've been putting off such as writing a letter, making a call, or attending a meeting.

- Become clear that memory glitches, pain, and death are not the enemy. Fear of them is.

- Find activities with heart and meaning for you.

- Bring mindfulness to everyday events like eating, walking, listening, petting an animal, and hugging a tree.

- Practice purposeful compassion toward others.

- Develop self-confidence in a way that is neither inflated nor deflated but filled with humility, hopefulness, and curiosity.

- Seek out means for enhancing your spirit.

- Ask your soul what still needs to be expressed.

- Nourish your senses; start with healing sounds, then receiving and giving caring touch, seeing beauty, and enjoying tastes and smells.

- Make an effort to learn something new each day.

- Wonder often.

- Exercise your mind by memorizing a saying or short poem; discuss an interesting topic with a friend; be fascinated with the world.

- Seek to be of service in some way.

- Cultivate friends of all ages.

- Mediate conflicts.

- Laugh out loud a lot.

- Be the sexy, zesty older person you were meant to be!

Eldership as a Revolutionary Endeavor

Energy self-care modalities will undoubtedly take their rightful place in mainstream health care given their ready efficacy for releasing distress and attaining high-level wellness. As working with *qi* becomes more known, energetic assessment and centering practices will likely be as much a part of future health care as taking blood pressure and regulating fluid balance.

Those of us who already have skills for self-healing with energy approaches will be able to assist others in need. Best of all, we will be able to hold fast to our focus and be able to center ourselves in the midst of the change and turbulence so evident in the world. Those of us with extended families or those living in communities will see opportunities for sharing what we have learned. As our consciousness evolves, engagement in human collective development becomes imperative.

Prominent biologists tell us that species evolve to meet the requirements of their environments. Carbon dioxide breathing organisms, for example, shifted millions of year ago to breathing oxygen as plant life on earth began producing an oxygen-rich atmosphere. The species who acquire habits of mutual aid are the fittest in the long run because they develop social structures for meeting the needs of their environments. For example, the difference between dogs and cats, both wild and domesticated, is that felines are solitary hunters while canines hunt in packs and have complex social structures that assign various tasks to the members of the clan. This enables canines to have more successful outcomes in hunting, reproduction, and family rearing. Primates generally have well-regulated societies in which cooperation is valued more highly than dominance.

"Survival of the fittest" as a philosophy does not work well in human society because it ignores social and planetary environments. It gives extraordinary powers to the wealthy few; it justifies exploitation of the living planet for the gain of the powerful. The distortions of massive planetary energy imbalance are all too apparent.[6]

As we survey the needs of the planet now, it's apparent that humans must evolve beyond self-orientation and special interests to find more synergistic, collaborative ways of thinking. As author Anodea Judith says, "The planet is dying from lack of heart, loss of soul."[7] As a species, we have not yet evolved to meet the vast issues facing us collectively.

Much of this book has suggested a stance of optimism and hope for facing life's challenges. Such a stance has to be suitable not only for the well-off, but also for the poor, the disadvantaged, and the vulnerable, lest it remain an elitist idea. A book, a course, or a healing method cannot resolve this issue, "rather it will be what we do as a nation to create conditions in which optimism can flower."[8]

One of my friends, sculptor Terry Davis, cares deeply about the exploitative logging and mining by multinational corporations in rural Oregon. To reach others too passive or resigned to face reality, he writes:

The people who play with countries

Like chips in games of roulette

Are shopping around

At a place near your town

For anything they can get.

Maybe we can stop them

Maybe we better try…

They're not easily satisfied

And our choices are slipping by.[9]

We are living in a time when involvement in social change is imperative. Change can only come with the focused efforts of those with the time and stalwart energy to work through thorny issues. Change also requires the vision of those who care about future generations and are not blindly invested in present gains. Enlightened elders with time and energy for real activism are an as-yet-untapped resource. Don't assume others will do the work of bringing about social change. Real elderhood is a revolutionary endeavor. We are the ones we have been waiting for!

Measures of Successful Aging

Author Stephen Levine describes growth into maturity as a lifelong process: "[G]rowth is…the art of falling down. Growth is measured by the gentleness and awareness with which we once again pick ourselves up, the lightness with which we dust ourselves off, the openness with which we continue and take the next unknown step, beyond our edge, beyond our holding, into the remarkable mystery of being. Going beyond the mind, we go beyond death. In the heart lies the deathless."[10]

How will you give meaning to the time you have now? What contribution can you make? What is the most important thing to remember as you look at completing your journey in the second half of life? Certainly, not just repeated household tasks, unceasing leisure, or interesting travel. Although these may be pleasant for a while, they do not nurture yearning for a meaningful life. Instead, they leave the soul empty and engender multiple attachments.

Ralph Waldo Emerson gave us a yardstick befitting our endeavor to measure successful aging: "To leave the world a bit better, whether by healthy child, a garden patch, or redeemed social condition; to know even one life has breathed easier because you live—that is to have succeeded."[11]

When we have done something to make the world a bit better, we connect to our art. This life is our creation. Every day is filled with choices that call for new generativity, and draw on the wellspring of our talents and gifts. Present events can become a source of learning, creativity, and involvement. Living within an anguished, confused world requires our full attention and willingness to keep evolving.

In the Irish tradition of giving blessings,[12] I conclude this time of sharing with a blessing to you:

May all your worry and anxiety about aging be transformed.

May you heal your life's wounds and harvest inner wisdom.

May the light of your soul greet you.

May you accept the wondrous gift of the timeless light within yourself!

Chapter Notes

Introduction

1. [S.D. Graham, "Interview with Jamie Lee Curtis," *AARP The Magazine* 51 (May–June 2008):3B, 63.

2. Editorial *AARP The Magazine* 27 (Jan.–Feb. 2008):1B, 88. Ten years ago, AARP dropped its original name of American Association of Retired People in favor of just the initials because so many elders actively work, consult, and volunteer in the second half of life. The organization's mission remains "To enhance the quality of life for everyone—those already in the second half of life and those headed there."

3. Statistics from *AARP Bulletin* (Jan.–Feb. 2008).

4. The concept of "audacious aging" was coined by author-publisher Dawson Church and is the title of a book published by his press, Elite Books (2008). See www.audaciousaging.com.

Chapter 1

1. NANDA International, *Nursing Diagnoses: Definitions and Classification*, Philadelphia, PA: NANDA-I, 2007: 332.

2. Many of the exercises given in this book are generic and from the author's study of movement to create energy shifts. Details are cited in D. Hover-Kramer, *Healing Touch: A guidebook for practitioners*, Albany, NY: Delmar/Thompson International, 2002.

3. For a further explanation of the energy of belief, see S. S. Bender and M. Sise, *The Energy of Belief: Psychology's power tools to focus intention and release blocking beliefs*, Santa Rosa, CA: Energy Psychology Press, 2008.

Chapter 2

1. For clinical case examples in which energy psychology treatments were used, see Dawson Church's website www.soulmedicineinstitute.org.

2. R. Gerber, *Vibrational Medicine*, Rochester, VT: Bear & Co., 2001: 101–106.

3. R. O. Becker, *Cross Currents*, New York: Tarcher/Putnam, 1990: 80.

4. Gerber, 171.

5. A. Cho and R. Stone, "Racing to capture darkness," *Science* 317: 32–34.

6. W. Tiller, *Science and Human Transformation*, Walnut Creek, CA: Pavoir, 1997.

7. A. Watson, "Quantum spookiness wins, Einstein loses in photon test" *Science* 277:481.

8. D. Radin, *Entangled Minds,* New York: Paraview, 2006; especially chapter on mind-matter interactions, pages 146–160.

9. Personal communications with Dr. Gaetan Chevalier, professor of research at California Institute for Human Science, Encinitas, CA, 2003–2006. See also H. Motoyama, *Theories of the Chakras,* Tokyo: Human Science Press, 2003.

10. *Science* (Aug 2001) *Epigenetics* special section, 293, 1064 on. Science (March 2008) *Epigenetics and gene regulation* special section, 319, and 1781 on.

11. H. Out, J.Dusek, T. Liberman, et al., "Genomic counter-stress changes induced by the relaxation response," *PLoS ONE,* retrieved online July 26, 2008.

12. D. Church, *The Genie in Your Genes,* Santa Rosa, CA: Elite Books, 2007: 44.

13. E. L. Rossi, *The Psychobiology of Gene Expression,* New York: W.W. Norton, 2002: 7.

14. C. Grauds and D. Childers, *The Energy Prescription,* New York: Bantam, 2005: 38.

15. Church, *The Genie in Your Genes,* 54–55.

16. www.therapeutictouch.com, www.healingtouchprogram.com, www.energy psych.org.

17. As reported by John Freedom, ACEP research committee director, ACEP certification training, Albuquerque, NM, May 21, 2008.

18. As reported by Dawson Church, ACEP research director, ACEP conference, Albuquerque, NM, May 17, 2008.

19. S. Wells, K. Polglase, H. B. Andrews, et al., "Evaluation of a meridian based intervention, emotional freedom techniques (EFT), for reducing specific phobias of small animals," *Journal of Clinical Psychology* 59:943–966.

20. J. E. Rowe, "The effects of EFT on long-term psychological symptoms," *Counseling and Clinical Psychology* 2:104–111.

21. P. G. Swingle, L. Pulos, and M. K. Swingle, "Neurophysiological indicators of EFT treatment of posttraumatic stress," *Subtle Energies and Energy Medicine* 15:75–86.

22. J. Andrade, "Energy psychology: Theory, indications, evidence," in D. Feinstein, *Energy Psychology Interactive: Rapid interventions for lasting change,* Ashland, OR: Innersource, 2004: 199–214.

23. P. Mollon, "Systemic review of the evidence base for energy psychology methods," in P. Mollon, *Psychoanalytic Energy Psychotherapy,* London: Karnac, 2007.

24. S. D. Peck, "The effectiveness of Therapeutic Touch (TT) for decreasing pain in elders with degenerative arthritis," *Journal of Holistic Nursing* 15:179–198.

25. P. Heidt, "Effects of TT on anxiety levels of hospitalized patients," *Nursing Research* 10:32–37.

26. M. Olson, N. Sneed, M. La Via et al., "Stress-induced immunosuppression and TT," *Alternative Therapies* 3:64–74. Also in J. Quinn and A. J. Strelkauskas, "Psychoimmunological effects of TT on practitioners and recently bereaved recipients," *Advances in Nursing Science* 15:13–26.

27. D. Wirth, "The effects of non-contact TT on the healing rate of full-thickness dermal wounds," *Journal of Subtle Energies* 1:1–20.

28. J. Quinn, "Holding sacred space: the nurse as healing environment," *Holistic Nursing Practice* 6:42-49. See also J. A. Stravena, "Therapeutic Touch coming of age," *Holistic Nursing Practice* 14:1–13.

Chapter 3

1. C. P. Monsanto, "Use of complementary and alternative medicine by older adults," *Complementary Health Practice Review* 11:27–46. D. Eisenberg and E. Hughes, "Report of first international conference on complementary, alternative and integrative medicine research" *Alternative Therapies* 7:101–112.

2. S. D. Peck, "The effectiveness of therapeutic touch for decreasing pain in elders with degenerative arthritis," *Journal of Holistic Nursing* 15: 176–198. See also P. Winstead-Fry and J. Kijek, "An integrative review and meta-analysis of TT research, *Alternative Therapies* 5:58–67.

3. Therapeutic Touch and Healing Touch organizations have a vast array of quantitative and qualitative research studies supporting energy-oriented therapies with chakra/biofield treatments. For specific, current details please see www.healingtouchprogram.com and www.therapeutictouch.com.

4. These concepts come from the author's twenty-eight years of experience in working with the chakras from a psychological perspective. Other authors will have slightly different perceptions. For a more complete discussion of the chakras, see also Hover-Kramer, *Creative Energies,* New York: W.W. Norton, 2002: 50–64.

5. The correspondence between chakra stimulation and colors visible to intuitive persons asl well as electromagnetic frequency emission studies is discussed more fully in V. Hunt, *Infinite Mind,* Malibu, CA: Malibu, 1995.

6. J. Levin, *God, Faith, and Health,* New York: John Wiley & Sons, 2001. H. G. Koenig, et al., "Religion, spirituality, and medicine: A rebuttal to skeptics," *International Journal of Psychiatry and Medicine* 29: 123–131.

7. E. H. Erikson, *Identity and the Life Cycle,* New York: W.W. Norton, 1959. See also E. H. Erikson, *The Life Cycle Completed,* New York: W.W. Norton, 1998.

8. For a complete listing of current research about acupoint therapy, see www.energypsych.org.

9. R. Gerber, *Vibrational Medicine*, Rochester, VT: Bear & Co., 2001: 122–127.

10. National Institutes of Health (Nov 1997); "Acupuncture," JAMA 280:1518-1524.

11. D. Feinstein, D. Eden, and G. Craig, *The Promise of Energy Psychology*, New York: Tarcher/Penguin, 2005: 28–64. See also www.emofree.com.

12. Some of the best-known works by Dr. Fred Gallo are *Energy Psychology*, Boca Raton, FL: CRC Press, 1998; *Energy Psychology in Psychotherapy*, New York: W.W. Norton, 2002; *Energy Diagnostic and Treatment Methods*, W.W. Norton, 2000; and *Energy Tapping for Trauma*, Oakland, CA: New Harbinger, 2007.

13. ACEP's website www.energypsych.org gives current conferences, trainings, and research. ACEP's newsletter is available by contacting ACEP administration, e-mail: info@energyspsych.org.

Chapter 4

1. R. Gerber, *Vibrational Medicine*, Rochester, VT: Bear & Co., 2001: 210.

2. D. Krieger, *Accepting Your Power to Heal*, Santa Fe, NM: Bear & Co., 1993: 65.

3. J. Astin, et al., "Mind-body medicine: State of the science, implications for practice," *Journal of the American Board of Family Practice* 18:131. See also J. A. Stravena, "Therapeutic Touch coming of age," *Holistic Nursing Practice* 14:1–13.

4. While this alignment is also well known in qigong, Barbara Brennan discusses the *hara* alignment and its link to setting intention in her book, *Light Emerging*, New York: Bantam, 1993: 287–s300.

5. P. E. Dennison and G. E. Dennison, *Brain Gym*, Glendale, CA: Edu-Kinesthetics, 1986: 31.

6. This is another hybrid derived predominantly from the Dennison's *Brain Gym*, 25–28. All of their exercises are exceedingly helpful in balancing the entire biofield as well as stimulating brain function in people of all ages.

Chapter 5

1. Although there are many documents describing similar exercises, the temporal tap is best described in Donna Eden's valuable book *Energy Medicine*, New York: Tarcher/Putnam, 1998: 332–s338.

Chapter 6

1. M. Seligman and M. Csikszentmihalyi, "Positive psychology: An introduction," *American Psychologist* 55:5. Also discussed at length in M. Seligman, *Authentic Happiness*, New York: Free Press, 2002.

2. D. Danner, D. Snowdon, and W. Friesen, "Positive emotions in early life and longevity: Findings from the nun study, *Journal of Personality and Social Psychology* 80:814.

Chapter 7

1. M. Ventura, "Beauty resurrected," *Psychotherapy Networker* 25:30–35.

2. A. Arrien, *The Second Half of Life,* Boulder, CO: Sounds True, 2006: 17.

3. M. H. Erickson, *My Voice Will Go with You,* ed. S. Rosen, New York: W. W. Norton, 1982.

Chapter 8

1. J. Hillman, *The Soul's Code,* New York: Random House, 1996).

2. Arrien, *The Second Half of Life,* 92.

3. M. Csikszentmihalyi, *Flow.* New York: Harper, 1991.

4. M. Csikszentmihalyi, *Creativity,* New York: HarperPerennial, 1996.

5. G. Kemperman and F. Gage, "New cells for the adult brain," *Scientific American* 280:48.

Chapter 9

1. I owe this image to Dr. Lee Pulos, Canadian author of many publications and active professor and therapist in his eighties. Personal communication at ACEP conference, Toronto, Canada, October 2007.

Chapter 10

1. C. G. Jung, *Memories, Dreams, Reflections,* New York: Vintage, 1965.

2. J. Fox, *Finding What You Didn't Lose,* New York: Putnam, 1995.

3. T. Rainer, *The New Diary,* Los Angeles, CA: J. P. Tarcher, 1978.

4. E. Berne, *Games People Play,* New York: Grove, 1964.

5. For further information, ACEP's website is www.energypsych.org.

Chapter 11

1. I am indebted to David C. Korten for articulating the nature of mature spirituality and showing how ethical behavior and social responsibility flow from it. See especially D. C. Korten, *The Great Turning,* San Francisco, CA: Berrett-Koehler, 2006: 262.

2. G. Ironson, H. Kremer, and D. Ironson, "Spirituality, spiritual experience, and spiritual transformation in the face of HIV," in J. D. Koss-Chioino and P. Hefner (eds.), *Spiritual Transformation and Healing,* Lanham, MD: Altamira, 2006.

3. D. Church, *The Genie in Your Genes,* Santa Rosa, CA: Elite Books, 2007: 172.

4. R. McCraty, M. Atkinson, and D. Tomasino, "Modulation of DNA conformation by hear-focused intention," Boulder Creek, CA: HeartMath Research Center, Institute of HeartMath, Publication #03-008.

5. L. Dossey, *Prayer Is Good Medicine,* New York: HarperCollins, 1997: 104.

6. W. B. Jonas, "The middle way: Realistic randomized controlled trials for the evaluation of spiritual healing," *Journal of Alternative and Complementary Medicine* 7:5–7.

7. J. Cameron, *The Artist's Way,* New York: Tarcher/Putnam, 1992: 163.

8. Haydn, as quoted in *American Chamber Music Periodical* (July 1999): 14.

Chapter 12

1. M. Seligman, *Authentic Happiness,* New York: Free Press, 2002: 32–35.

2. M. J. T. Stepanek, *Heartsongs,* New York: Hyperion, 2001.

3. V. Frankl, *Man's Search for Meaning,* New York: Pocket Books, 1984: 86–87.

4. S. Hermes, "The relevance of art in personal growth among Native Americans," doctoral dissertation (2003), Antioch College; and personal communications in 2003.

5. M. Lerner, "Surviving the Bush and Sharon years," *Tikkun* (March–April 2001).

Chapter 13

1. International Academy of Compounding Pharmacists, www.iacprx.org; accessed 2008.

2. 2004 statistic from American Chronic Pain Association, Rocklin, CA.

3. L. Lind and K. Swarts, *Pain Management Toolkit,* Medford, OR: Heartwork Productions, 2008.

4. M. Phillips, *Reversing Chronic Pain,* Berkeley, CA: North Atlantic Books, 2007.

5. S. D. Peck, "The effectiveness of Therapeutic Touch for decreasing pain in elders with degenerative arthritis," *Journal of Holistic Nursing* 15:179–198. V. Slater, "Energetic healing," in B. M. Dossey, L Keegan, and C. E. Guzzetta, *Holistic Nursing,* Gaithersburg, MD, Aspen Publishers, 2000. D. W. Wardell and K. Weymouth, "Review of studies of Healing Touch," *Journal of Nursing Scholarship* 36:147–154.

6. D. Feinstein, D. Eden, and G. Craig, *The Promise of Energy Psychology,* New York: Tarcher/Penguin, 2005: 227-8.

7. Hover-Kramer, D., *Healing Touch,* Albany, NY: Delmar/Thompson International, 2002: 231.

8. J. Dillard, *The Chronic Pain Solution,* New York: Bantam, 2003: 33.

Chapter 14

1. M. Olson and B. M. Dossey, "Dying in peace" in B. M. Dossey, L Keegan, and C. E. Guzzetta (eds.), *Holistic Nursing,* Sudbury, MA: Jones and Bartlett, 2005.

2. L. Dossey, *Healing Words,* San Francisco, CA: HarperSanFrancisco, 1993: 206, 209.

3. R. Moody, *Reflections on Life after Life,* New York: Bantam, 1978.

4. L. M. Daggett, "Continued encounters: The experience of after-death communication," *Journal of Holistic Nursing* 23:191–207.

5. S. Michael, "Integrating chronic illness into one's life" *Journal of Holistic Nursing* 14:251–267.

6. L. Thornton, "Holistic nursing and integrative palliative care," *Journal of Holistic Nursing* 27:3,16.

7. D. W. Wardell, "Using Healing Touch for end of life care," *Beginnings: American Holistic Nurses Association* 27:28–29.

8. P. G. Stover, "Surviving to share," *Beginnings: American Holistic Nurses Association* 28:20–21.

9. E. Kübler-Ross, *Death: The final stage of growth.* Englewood Cliffs, NJ: Prentice-Hall, 1975.

Chapter 15

1. J. Campbell and B. Moyers, *The Power of Myth,* New York: Doubleday, 1988.

2. J. Briggs and F. D. Peat, *Seven Life Lessons of Chaos,* New York: HarperCollins, 2000:32.

3. D. Ornish, *Love and Survival,* New York: HarperPerennial, 1999.

4. M. E. McCullough, et al., "Religious involvement and mortality: A meta review," *Health Psychology* 19:211–s222.

5. D. Gruder, *The New IQ,* Santa Rosa, CA: Elite Books, 2007.

6. D. C. Korten, *The Great Turning,* San Francisco, CA: Berrett-Koehler, 2006.

7. A. Judith, *Waking the Global Heart,* Santa Rosa, CA: Elite Books, 2006.

8. L. Dossey, *The Extraordinary Healing Power of Ordinary Things.* New York: Harmony Books, 2006.

9. Retrieved from e-mail communication with Terry Davis, May 21, 2008, reprinted with permission and from personal communication.

10. S. Levine, *Meetings at the Edge,* New York: Anchor, 1984: xiv.

11. Emerson quoted in A. Arrien, *The Second Half of Life,* Boulder, CO: Sounds True, 2006: 152.

12. J. O'Donohue, *To Bless the Space Between Us,* New York: Doubleday, 2008.

Glossary

Acedia—soul killing patterns such as boredom, apathy, not caring, stagnation, loneliness, or indifference. Acedia signals that generative energy is blocked and gene expression is limited.

Acupoint—a node or point along a meridian pathway that has slightly less electricalresistance than other parts of the meridian and serves as a minute relay for electrical energy along the meridian. Most meridians have numerous acupoints.

Acupressure—a method of working with the meridians through direct pressure, tapping, or holding on an acupoint. Meridian-based psychotherapy is a form of emotional acupressure.

Acupuncture—a method known in ancient China for more than five thousand years to aid the body in restoring balance. Stimulation of acupoints is accomplished by insertion of fine needles or the use of heat or herbs.

Aura—metaphysical term for the human energy field or biofield.

Balancing—term used to describe the realignment of the biofield to its natural symmetrical and vibrational potential.

Biofield—scientific term for the vibrational emanations surrounding and extending beyond the human body. The biofield can be measured by SQID (super-conducting quantum interference device) and sensed by skilled health-care practitioners.

Centering—the process of focusing one's attention and intention to be fully present to the moment. In health care, centering refers to the process of setting intention on behalf of another person and setting aside personal issues and outcome expectations.

Chakra—one of seven major human energy centers that spin like rotating vortices (chakra means "spinning wheel" in Sanskrit).

Chakras are also called the centers of consciousness, as they relate to psychological and developmental properties in the person.

Clearing—releasing, letting go, smoothing, or unruffling the biofield. Hand movements above the biofield can facilitate release of energy blockage or negative emotions.

Creativity—the innate generativity, the capacity for innovation and inventiveness in all humans.

Desired beliefs—productive and functional beliefs resulting in higher levels of creativity and joy; example: "I am a loveable and capable person."

Disease—aka *dis-ease,* or the absence of health. In current medical practice, disease refers to the presence of pathological symptoms that need to be removed. In energy psychology, disease is a feedback signal pointing to energetic imbalance as its source.

Energy blockage—term describing the constriction of natural flow patterns in the human energy system; may refer to a depleted or closed chakra, asymmetry in the biofield, or nonpolarity and reversal in the meridian pathways.

Energy center—synonym for chakra; human energy vortex.

Energy healing—broad term used to describe the use of interventions that release energy blockage or imbalance, followed by repatterning, balancing, and aligning the human subtle energies to higher levels of functioning.

Energy psychology—interventions to release emotional distress and increase self-efficacy by using the resources of the human energy resources such as the biofield, the chakras, and the meridian acupoints.

Focusing—holding positive intention for creating inner harmony and peacefulness. Focusing can be enhanced by bringing hands to a specific part of the body or subtle energy field.

Grounding—connecting to the earth and earth's energy field to calm the mind and bring balance to one's energy system.

Healing—ongoing evolution toward higher levels of awareness and functioning; movement toward high levels of well-being and health.

Health—unimpeded personal mind-body-spirit communication for peace and wholeness. In energy psychology, health refers to the presence of strong *qi*, inner fire and vitality, that transforms toxins, promotes gene expression, and brings nourishment to each cell. In current medical practice, health means the absence of definable disease.

Human energy system—also known as the human vibrational matrix; the entire interactive dynamic of human subtle energies. The system consists of the multidimensional field, the chakras, the meridians, and related acupoints, as well as other subtle energy flow pathways.

Intention—holding one's inner awareness and focus to accomplish a goal or achieve connecting communication; a specific form of directed consciousness such as prayer or meditation.

Limiting belief—a counterintention to one's stated volition, which may be in conscious awareness or held in the subconscious mind. Such a belief interferes with achieving one's full potential. Examples: "I'm not capable; I can't do anything right."

Mantra—a repeated self-affirming, positive statement.

Nocebo—a powerful negative message; often given by physicians when stating a diagnosis of serious illness without possible mitigation or hope.

Placebo—from the Latin for "I stand in place," a powerful positive message that stands in the place of emotional distress. Example: enhancing well-being by repeating positive affirmations or mantras, using helpful imagery to reduce anxiety.

Psychoenergetic balancing—interventions that interrelate psychological insights with understanding of human energy resources.

Psychoenergetic disturbance—a pervasive distortion in the human energy system that is both psychological and energetic in nature but may or may not have physical aspects.

Qi—pronounced "chee" and also written as chi or ch'i; traditional Chinese medicine term for the vital life force.

Subtle energy—term proposed by Einstein to explain discrete emanations that radiate from living organisms and constantly interact with matter.

Tapping—repeated percussive stimulation of an acupoint to enhance its full function. Stimulation of an acupoint can also be achieved by holding it, putting pressure on it, or using internal imagery.

Transpersonal—term coined by Drs. Abraham Maslow, Anthony Sutich, and Stanislav Grof, founders of the Association for Transpersonal Psychology, to describe psychospiritual realms beyond the personal.

Universal energy field—term used by many healers such as Barbara Brennan and Rosalyn Bruyere to describe the sources of unlimited energy that surround and interpenetrate all aspects of the universe. In our solar system, the sun is a representation of this unlimited energy source.

Unruffling—term coined by Dolores Krieger, PhD, founder of Therapeutic Touch, to suggest the clearing or smoothing of a ruffled, disturbed area of the biofield.

Recommendations for Further Reading

Arrien, A. *The Second Half of Life: Opening the eight gates of wisdom*. Boulder, CO: Sounds True, 2007.

Badonsky, J. *The Nine Modern Day Muses (and a Bodyguard)*. New York: Gotham Books, 2003.

Burkhardt, M. A., and M. G. Nagai-Jacobson. Spirituality: *Living our connectedness*. Albany, NY: Delmar/Thompson Learning, 2002.

Campbell, J., with B. Moyers. *The Power of Myth*. New York: Doubleday, 1988.

Church, D. *The Genie in Your Genes: Epigenetic medicine and the new biology of intention*. Santa Rosa, CA: Elite Books, 2007.

Csikszentmihalyi, M. *Creativity: Flow and the psychology of discovery and invention*. New York: HarperCollins, 1996.

Dass, Ram. *Still Here: Embracing Aging, Changing, and Dying*. New York: Riverhead Books, 2000.

Dossey, L. *Healing Words: The power of prayer and the practice of medicine*. San Francisco, CA: HarperSanFrancisco, 1993.

Dossey, L. *Reinventing Medicine*. Francisco, CA: HarperSanFrancisco, 1999.

Dossey, L. *The Extraordinary Healing Power of Ordinary Things. Fourteen natural steps to health and happiness*. New York: Harmony Books, 2006.

Fox, J. *Finding What You Didn't Lose: Expressing your truth and creativity through poem-making*. New York: Putnam, 1995.

Fox, M. *Sins of the Spirit, Blessings of the Flesh: Lessons for transforming evil in soul and society*. New York: Harmony Books, 1999.

Gruder, D. *The New IQ: How integrity intelligence serves you, your relationships, and our world*. Santa Rosa, CA: Elite Books, 2008.

Hillman, J. *The Soul's Code: In search of character and calling*. New York: Random House, 1996.

Hover-Kramer, D. *Creative Energies: Integrative energy psychotherapy for self-expression and healing*. New York: W.W. Norton, 2002.

Hover-Kramer, D. *Healing Touch: A guidebook for practitioners*. Albany, NY: Delmar/Thompson International, 2002.

Judith, A. *Waking the Global Heart: Humanity's rite of passage from the love of power to the power of love*. Santa Rosa, CA: Elite Books, 2006.

Kandel, E. R. *In Search of Memory: The emergence of a new science of mind*. New York: W.W. Norton, 2007.

Kornfield, J. *The Art of Forgiveness, Lovingkindness, and Peace.* New York: Bantam, 2002.

Korten, D. C. *The Great Turning: From empire to earth community.* San Francisco, CA: Berrett-Koehler, 2006.

Kushner, H. S. *Living a Life that Matters.* New York: Anchor, 2002.

Levine, S. *Healing into Life and Death.* Garden City, NY: Anchor Press/ Doubleday, 1987.

Macy, J., and M. Young Brown. *Coming Back to Life: Practices to reconnect our lives, our world.* Stony Creek, CT: New Society, 1998.

O'Donohue, J. *Beauty: The invisible embrace.* New York: HarperCollins, 2004.

O'Donohue, J. *To Bless the Space Between Us: A book of blessings.* New York: Doubleday, 2008.

Ornish, D. *Love and Survival: The scientific basis for the healing power of intimacy.* New York: HarperPerennial, 1999.

Oschman, J. L. *Energy Medicine: The scientific basis.* Edinburgh, UK: Churchill Livingstone/Harcourt, 2000.

Page, C. *Spiritual Alchemy: How to transform your life.* London: Random House UK, 2005.

Pipher, M. *Another Country: Navigating the emotional terrain of our elders.* New York: Riverhead Books, 1999.

Radin, D. *Entangled Minds: Extrasensory experiences in a quantum reality.* New York: Paraview Pocket Books, 2006.

Rossi, E. L. *The Psychobiology of Gene Expression: Neuroscience and neurogenesis in hypnosis and the healing arts.* New York: W.W. Norton, 2002.

Seligman, M. *Authentic Happiness: Using the new positive psychology to realize your potential for lasting fulfillment.* New York: Free Press, 2002.

Simon, D. *Return to Wholeness: Embracing body, mind, and spirit in the face of cancer.* New York: Wiley, 1999.

Spencer, R. L. *The Craft of the Warrior.* Berkeley, CA: Frog Books, 2005.

Organizational Resources

AARP (American Association for Retired People)
601 E Street NW
Washington, DC 20049
Phone: 888-687-2277
Website: www.aarp.org

American Holistic Nurses Association
323 N. San Francisco Street, Suite 201
Flagstaff, AZ 86001
Phone: 800-278-2462
Website: www.ahna.org

Association for Comprehensive Energy Psychology (ACEP)
349 West Lancaster Avenue, Suite 101
Haverford, PA 19401
Phone: 619-861-2237
Website: www.energypsych.org
E mail: acep_ed@energypsych.org

Healing Touch Program (HTP)
P.O. Box 16189
Golden, CO 80402
Phone: 303-989-0581
Website: www.healingtouchprogram.com
E-mail: Cynthia@Healintouchprogram.com

International Society for the Study of Subtle Energies and Energy Medicine (ISSSEEM)
11005 Ralston Road, Suite 210
Arvada, CO 80004
Phone: 303-425-4625
Website: www.issseem.org

Soul Medicine Institute
c/o Dawson Church
PO Box 442
Fulton, CA 95439
Phone: 707-525-9292
E-mail: dawson@authorspublishing.com
Website: www.soulmedicineinstitute.com
and www.epigeneticmedicine.org

Therapeutic Touch
Nurse Healers—Professional Associates International
1184 Route 4
Craryville, NY 12521
Phone: 877-32-NHPAI
E-mail: nhpai@therapeutic-touch.org
Website: www.therapeutic-touch.org

Index